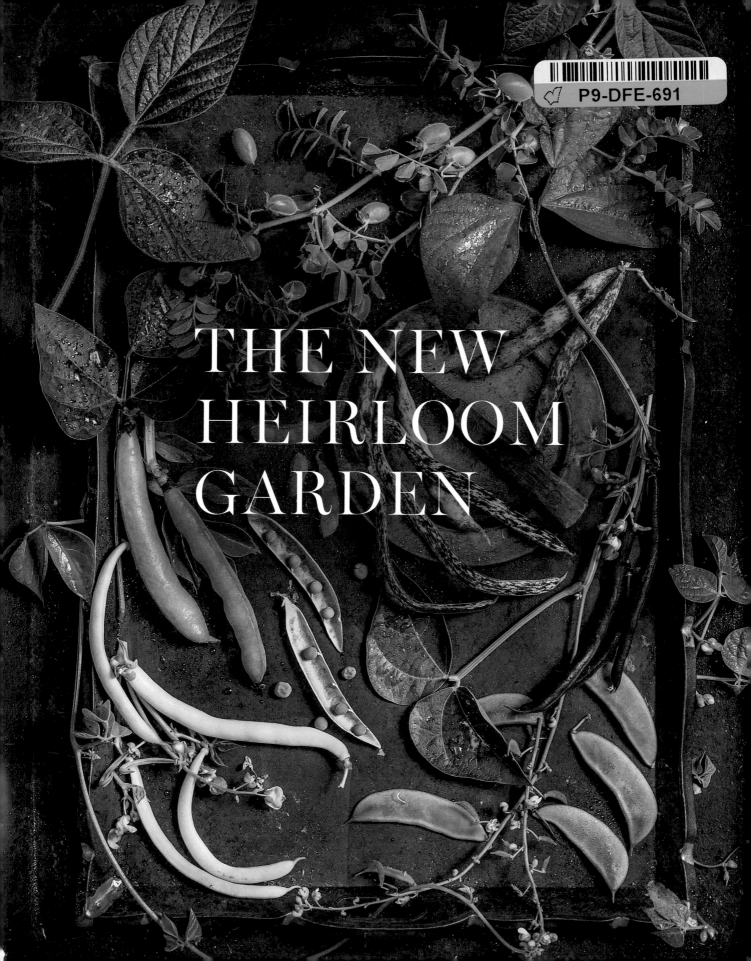

THE NEW HEIRLOOM GARDEN

THE NEW HEIRLOOM GARDEN

DESIGNS, RECIPES, AND
HEIRLOOM PLANTS FOR COOKS
WHO LOVE TO GARDEN

ELLEN ECKER OGDEN

PHOTOGRAPHS BY MATTHEW BENSON

RODALE

For my grandson, Liam Fredrik Schuster

"It is spring again.
The earth is like a child that
knows poems by heart."
—Rainer Maria Rilke

Contents

HEIRLOOM GARDEN DESIGNS

DIGGING DEEPER
WITH PLANT FAMILIES AND RECIPES

INTRODUCTION

THE ART OF GROWING FOOD

"Here, try one of these," I'll say when you visit my heirloom garden, offering you a handful of sugar snap peas, a sprig of chervil to tingle your taste buds, or a sweet Fraises des Bois strawberry. "Look at this!" I'll say, as I carefully peel away the deep mahogany leaves of a fall Treviso radicchio and pluck off a bitter leaf, or "Smell this," as I point out a vanilla-scented white nicotiana.

I may be able to entice you to try something new from my kitchen garden, but digging deeper in search of the old-fashioned varieties, those delicate fruits, fragrant flowers, and open-pollinated heirloom vegetables, is the secret to unearthing your own favorites and establishing a lifelong desire to grow a food garden. And it all starts with a seed. Watching green shoots emerge from the ground—active, robust, and alive—is proof that seeds are pre-equipped with everything they need to send forth a root, a shoot, and a leaf. All I need to do is insert them into the soil, step back, and watch.

Why we garden is as individual as the plants themselves—for food, for beauty, to escape, or simply for exercise. Yet we all start with the same three things—seeds, plants, and soil—and each of our gardens will be completely unique. I planted my first garden fresh out of art school and just after starting a graphic design business. It was a way to blend the colors and textures of plants with my love of cooking and eating.

It would be stretching the truth to say my first garden thrived. There was a constant battle with the weeds, and the garden hose didn't quite reach, so the plants were frequently thirsty. Yet the thrill of dashing to the garden just before dinner to clip a basket of baby artichokes and a fistful of cosmos kept me at it. I reveled in fewer trips to the grocery store in favor of planting everything I might eat throughout the year. It gave me immense satisfaction to know I was part of the natural cycle of the seasons that made up a year in the garden, and it still does.

Back then, I didn't know that starting with a design could make a difference in the way I felt about my garden. At the time, it actually felt like a lot of work to get out into the garden and not much fun. Working along with my husband, the goal was to grow as much as we could to feed our family of four, which meant that I'd spend the entire month of August standing at the stove, canning and freezing beans, spinach, and broccoli. At the sign of the first frost, we'd harvest potatoes and place them in the root cellar along with cabbage, kohlrabi, leeks, beets, and carrots packed in sand. It was more a way of life that allowed us to live off the land, as stewards and recipients of healthy organic food.

In 2003, my relationship to the garden changed when I moved from the ten-acre farm to a smaller plot in a village setting. With neighbors on either side and less than a quarter acre, it was a challenge to transfer my garden skills from a large Victory garden style to something more compact. It required me to think small, which is how I discovered the art of growing food. Instead

TEN REASONS TO GROW AN HEIRLOOM GARDEN

The best-tasting vegetables are heirlooms.

The most-fragrant flowers are heirlooms.

The most-interesting plants are heirlooms.

Heirlooms produce healthy nectar and pollen for pollinators.

Heirlooms have a natural tolerance for regional conditions.

Heirloom seeds can be saved year after year.

Heirloom plants can be grafted and come true.

Heirlooms preserve the biodiversity of our food system.

Heirlooms provide a way to re-create history through historical gardens.

Heirlooms have great names and offer good stories and memories.

of growing everything I would need for a full year, I reduced my plant wish list to only those foods that I could not buy at the local farmers' market or through a CSA (community-supported agriculture). The plants and flowers I chose to grow reflected my vintage 1905 house, which involved growing and rediscovering heirlooms.

I started with a five-year plan, mapping out my future garden areas by first taking note of what was already growing. There was an antique apple tree in the backyard and two overgrown heirloom lilacs on either side of the porch. Knowing nothing about garden design, I took day trips to visit gardens through the Garden Conservancy's Open Days tours, returning home with lists of plants and design sketches in an attempt to organize my landscape. What surprised me most about these forays to visit beautiful gardens was that many of the most elegant gardeners grew only ornamentals. Edible gardens either did not exist or were kept far out of sight, behind a barn or garage, often sadly neglected.

I garden because I love to eat. It's that simple, and it became my goal to teach myself how to design kitchen gardens, at least partly in order to make it more inviting to be in the garden and turn "work" into "play." The way to do this was to create simple designs that transformed growing food into something fun and engaging, rather than feeling like effort. In 2011, my book *The Complete Kitchen Garden* was published, with twelve kitchen garden designs that were both beautiful and productive, along with recipes to inspire the cook to plant a seed, watch it grow, and then sit down at the table to the full satisfaction of eating from his or her own garden.

Good gardeners make growing a garden look easy, but gardening takes time, experience, and an eye for plant material and placement, which is why starting with the basics and a solid plan makes sense. We all want that weed-free, everblooming, overflowing harvest-basket type of garden, yet, in fact, gardening starts by getting dirty and devoting time to tasks that are not always rewarding. When growing a food garden, try to think about how it is more than a place to grow food. It can heighten your awareness on every level and become a place that taps into all of the senses; we inhale more deeply, look more closely, taste with appreciation, listen with curiosity, and touch everything.

With this new book, I offer more of my kitchen garden designs and recipes, with a focus on heirloom varieties in order to bring back the best-tasting vegetables, the most-fragrant flowers, and the forgotten fruits that grow in your backyard. Perhaps you'll be inspired to dig more deeply into why heirlooms are important for protecting biodiversity, to listen to the stories, to learn more about the politics of seeds, to meet experts in the field, and to think more about how you can become a seed saver. Seeds may look small, but they hold a lot of power and lore.

You may have a one-square-foot plot rubbing shoulders with a kitchen door or a wilderness waiting to be tamed, but planting a garden of any size is an opportunity to dig deeper into the past, to rediscover older varieties that have largely been dropped from the seed catalogs, to change the way we have been gardening for the past century, and to turn back the clock to pay attention to why seeds matter in the long run.

In a world where most supermarket options have largely dulled our palates and choices are homogenized, food gardens are more important than ever. Tasting food pulled from the ground and twisting off a green stem, or picking up an apple dropped from a tree at the peak of ripeness, is the way I wish we all ate. A true garden settles into a space where the garden and home merge, becoming an extension of you, opening the senses in new and inspiring ways, and ultimately creating a sanctuary for living. An heirloom garden is an opportunity to plant a piece of history that provides a deeper connection to the food you eat, the people you love, and the landscape that surrounds your home.

— Ellen Ecker Ogden

STEP BY STEP

ELEMENTS FOR A SUCCESSFUL DESIGN

ACCORDING TO ANCIENT CELTIC LORE, it is best to knock two rocks together, speak to the earth, and state your intention before you dig into the ground or make any changes at all to the landscape. Offer a humble prayer, then proceed with care and dignity. In that tradition, you are connecting with the existing landscape, as a way to leave behind a longer legacy than your present moment.

I believe in taking this a step further, to thoughtfully step back and first plan out a landscape to see how everything links together. Our backyards, the plants we choose to grow, and how the landscape is designed are about creating a sanctuary for all living creatures. This requires a thoughtful step-by-step process, attention to detail, curiosity, and the patience to hold a vision that will ultimately transform your backyard into an heirloom landscape.

START WITH A LONG-TERM PLAN, or even just a five-year plan, as a means of looking forward, and eventually looking back. It will allow you to stay focused on the future goal of creating a well-designed landscape and to enjoy the process and the end product more fully. Rather than jump in with a quick start, digging holes or moving trees, take time to sit in the garden area, decide how much space to devote to a garden, and what to plant when. As you begin to visualize, you may find that the design for your garden will start to unfold in your mind's eye. This is the beginning of a conversation you will ultimately have with everything that is already growing on your land and all around you, as you merge old designs and plants with new.

Before you start to change anything, draw out your vision on a piece of graph paper, beginning with a bird's-eye view of your property to grasp the big picture. Outline the boundaries, noting the four cardinal directions: east, west, north, and south. Notice where the sun comes up in the morning, how it casts shadows during the day, and where it sets at night. Mark where the house sits on the property, the driveway, and any permanent obstacles that interfere with a garden, including existing trees, shrubs, and underground septic tanks. Then close your eyes and visualize that you are a bird flying above, taking in your land and how it connects to that of your neighbors and

1

LANDSCAPE OVERVIEW

THE FIVE-YEAR PLAN

the larger community. Then put it all down on graph paper and keep adding to it each year to document your progress.

The five-year plan slows down your pace, and it builds a deeper, more satisfying connection to your garden with the overall landscape at the heart. Connecting all the dots and paying attention to how plants, trees, wildlife, and people interact goes beyond the physical act of constructing a garden. Create a garden that provides the feeling of a sanctuary; find that sweet spot that draws you outdoors to sit and savor the potential of all that your landscape has to offer, both now and in the future.

These may all seem like daunting decisions when you first get started, yet when you thoughtfully plot out the design on paper, it becomes easier to imagine how everything will fit together as a whole.

2

PENCIL TO PAPER

INSPIRATION

NOW THAT YOU HAVE THE LARGE OVERVIEW on paper, it's time to zoom in on the garden design. Each new design starts typically with a shape, figuring out the angle of the beds and how the design sits with the house, looking at where the paths join, and siting the garden shed and placing a bench. Start at the front door and move around to all sides of your house, looking at your landscape as a whole unit.

Drawing is a creative practice, and before a drawing emerges it may take staring at a blank piece of paper for a long time, pencil in hand. If this happens, trigger the visuals by paging through garden books and magazines or visiting other gardens for ideas. Visiting public gardens, private gardens, or simply driving around your neighborhood to see what other people are growing can jump-start ideas. In order to become a writer, you need to be a reader to learn a vocabulary, and the same is true with gardening: you need to fine-tune your sense of design to know what you like in order to bring it home.

Whenever I start to draw a new design, it takes three tries: the first is formal and safe, typically based on a familiar four-square approach and always very geometric. Then a second design emerges that is curvy and a little bit wilder. By the time the third design emerges, it is a combination of both, and it's usually the one I pick because it has input from both the left and right sides of the brain. The key to drawing is not to think about it too hard; something will surface that will allow you to ultimately say, "Aha!"

Choose one of the designs in this book, mix and match to fit your style and your landscape, or start fresh with your own. Once you have a design on paper, double-check your measurements on the graph paper and then plot it again outside to make sure it fits.

3

STICKS AND TWINE

PAPER TO SOIL

NOW THAT YOU HAVE CHOSEN YOUR SPOT and plotted your design on paper, it's time to take the paper dream to reality—outdoors. Measuring out the garden with sticks and twine is a surefire method that allows you to visualize the garden before you start digging and to be sure it is exactly what you have in mind.

With measurements in hand, take a flexible tape measure, two dozen small stakes, and a large ball of twine into the yard. Measure it out, pound a stake into each outside corner of the garden boundary, and wrap twine around each stake to establish the perimeter. Continue working inward, measuring the center of each side. Wrap twine around each stake to create the central axis and focal point.

Next, establish the entrance and main pathways by measuring 2 feet in either direction from the center, creating a wide central path that is 4 feet wide. Once the general outlines are established, step back to look at the finished space.

It might not actually look or feel the way you had visualized it on paper, which is why this exercise is critical before you begin to dig or build. Keep adjusting the design, looking at it from all angles. Set up a bench inside or nearby, pretend with large pots that can substitute for plants, and generally test out the space in your imagination until you are sure it is right. Go inside and look at how you will view the garden from your windows. Will the garden be equally engaging both in summer, full of plants, and in winter?

This is my method, yet there are plenty of other ways to do this preliminary planning. If I am designing a garden in the winter and the outside is frozen tundra, I'll stretch masking tape across the floor or indoor carpet to measure the space, and use pillows to stand in for plants. Taking time to get it right makes all the difference because, as with building a house, the more planning you do up front, the better the space will work for you in the long run.

THE BONES

GARDEN PATHS

IT'S TEMPTING TO IGNORE THE PATHS in a design by simply leaving enough space in between the rows to move around and through the beds. Yet paths are not only the "bones" of the garden but they also play a long-term role in its function and beauty. Paths can be straight or curved, yet they define the shape and structure of the garden all year round.

Choosing the best material for lining paths will contribute to your comfort and the way the garden works visually. The main path should always be 4 feet wide, enough for two people to walk side by side. In and around the garden, narrow auxiliary paths that are 2 feet wide are enough for weeding and harvest.

In the old days, garden paths were often composed of the soil in between the rows, yet this meant more weeding. Planning the way the paths integrate with the beds and selecting a path material to keep weeds down will make the garden design more inviting. Choosing the right path material can take trial and error—yet it can be easily changed over time.

HERE ARE SOME OPTIONS TO CONSIDER:

HAY OR STRAW

A simple, straightforward, and natural choice for a garden path is natural hay or straw. If you live near the ocean, salt-marsh hay or seaweed is an excellent choice, too. The biggest advantage of this medium is availability and convenience, plus cleanup at the end of the season involves sweeping it up and topping off the compost pile with it. Disadvantages are that hay can contain weed seeds, and both hay and straw can harbor hiding places for slugs or snakes. But either is a great way to keep weeds from sprouting and to keep boots clean after a rainstorm.

GRASS

A lush runway of green grass looks luxurious yet may not be the best environmental choice, considering irrigation needs. Grass paths require maintenance to keep them edged, watered, and mowed, and they're not a sound option if you live in a drought-prone area. Grass also takes up nitrogen from the soil to stay green, and it can easily creep into the beds unless they are edged with a steel barrier or raised to keep the roots from invading.

BARK MULCH Natural bark mulch is the most common weed barrier in garden beds and paths, often used in combination with landscape cloth underneath, yet it also is not the best choice for the environment, especially when purchased in plastic bags or if used with plastic cloth as a barrier. Try to find a local source of wood chips and paper landscape cloth, and use them only on pathways. Bark mulch works for only a few years before the weeds will creep back in through any gaps, and it becomes harder each year to keep it tidy. Bark is inexpensive and good for the first few years in a new garden, but consider replacing it with a different material over time. Choose natural-color brown over dyed mulch.

GRAVEL The satisfying crunch of gravel beneath your feet is one of the many reasons I favor this option, plus it stays in place and looks good over a long period of time. It's also a great way to keep the bottoms of your shoes clean, especially after a heavy rain. Gravel comes in different colors and sizes, depending on your location, so try to find a local source rather than shipping stones across the country. In coastal areas, crushed shells offer a crisp white to accentuate the colors in the garden. Inquire with your garden landscaper or garden center for local sources of available gravel and options for sizes; try it in a section to see what you prefer.

FLAT STONE Large natural stones are a good way of grounding the space between the beds or, if they are set into gravel, forming stepping-stones and offering landing pads for your feet. Choose stones that either match those you already have around your yard or in the natural geography to ensure continuity. To avoid tripping or stubbing toes, dig the stones in with a shovel to set them into the soil flush with the natural contours of the land (or hire a good mason to do so).

5

TERRA FIRMA

SOIL

SOIL IS THE KEY COMPONENT of any successful garden, whether you are growing food or flowers. Good soil feeds your plants and, when growing food, ultimately feeds you. Keep it organic, weed-free, and nutrient-rich, plus make sure it has tilth, or good texture, with small pockets for air and water. Buying bags of soil for your garden may seem like a convenient option, yet it's akin to buying fast food. Most bagged soils generally lack necessary nutrients to sustain plants over time and often come with built-in fertilizer to replace the natural micronutrients available in compost.

GARDEN SOIL

Healthy soil supports a strong root system, holds plants upright, and absorbs and retains water. It should smell slightly sweet and hold together when squeezed, like a good chocolate cake. When plants lack proper nutrients from the soil, they are more prone to disease and pests, so paying attention to your soil from the start will give your plants an advantage.

Before tractors and rototillers, every gardener owned a garden fork to turn the soil. Mechanical churning of the soil can lead to breaking up the fine membranes and microorganisms that comprise the structure of the soil. Learn to work with your soil, add compost, and plant cover crops in between seasons that will naturally provide organic materials. This will lead to better health for your soil, higher nutrients in the food you grow, and stronger stems for your cutting garden.

POTTING SOIL

Gearing up for the growing season often starts with a bag or two of potting soil to start seedlings or fill containers, yet bagged soil can vary greatly, depending on the brand. Take your time to look and compare before grabbing the cheapest one you can find, and make sure you are getting the right stuff.

Garden soil is heavy and dense, and will not be ideal for containers, starting seeds, or raising seedlings, because new roots prefer a looser, finer mix. There is a difference between starting mix, which is made from ingredients such as peat moss, perlite, coconut fiber, and vermiculite, and potting soil, which often contains mostly peat moss with a slow-release fertilizer or moisture-retention granules that expand and absorb water. If you are a purely organic gardener, you probably do not want these additives in your garden soil. Many organic gardeners prefer to make their own potting soil by combining one-third sphagnum peat moss; one-third compost that has been sifted through a large-mesh screen to remove sticks, stones, and large chunks that are not fully decomposed; and one-third vermiculite or sand, plus a cup of worm castings for every 5-gallon bucket of soil mix.

6

ORGANIC FERTILIZER

COMPOST AND COVER CROPS

COMPOST INVOLVES THE RECYCLING of naturally decomposing materials that provide nutrients to your garden soil; in other words, what comes from the garden goes back to the garden, keeping food scraps out of the landfill. Compost works because of microorganisms and worms that heat up and dig deep, helping the soil renew some of the nutrients that are removed when food and flowers are grown.

The best way to start a compost pile is to set up a bucket or bowl near the kitchen sink and start collecting eggshells, coffee grounds, trimmings from vegetables, banana peels, old bread, and almost anything that is edible, although it's best to avoid dairy and meat scraps.

Construct a bin system outside, preferably a two- or three-bin arrangement with one open side contained by wire mesh so that air can flow to create composting action; for the front, use slats that can be removed when turning the pile with a garden fork. Locate the compost bins near the garden but away from the house, perhaps on the other side of a short fence or row of trees yet in direct or dappled sunlight.

Start the pile by laying down a few stalks from sunflowers or small branches, just to give the base a little airspace. Then begin to fill the bin with layers of green and brown, as if you were making lasagna. Green is the spent plant materials from the garden, the lawn clippings, and any food scraps; brown is straw, hay, and/or leaves. If you keep chickens or rabbits, wood chips from their bedding can be used in the brown layer.

Compost that is not properly layered will not heat adequately and can start to release odors. The bacteria responsible for breaking down food scraps are especially active when combined with fresh air, which is why it is key not to just let it sit to decompose but to actively take a part in its making. Turn everything once a week with a garden fork to encourage the naturally occurring heat and to break up the material.

As compost breaks down, it will release micronutrients that create a healthy tonic of rich humus, which contributes to your soil's nutrition and overall structure. When starting the garden in spring, plan to spread a thin layer of compost on both vegetable and flower beds. Midsummer, use a handful of compost to spread around the base of all your plants, which will give the roots another boost. In the fall, if you still have compost to spread, finish the season with another thin layer to keep the soil nourished throughout the winter.

The kitchen and basic yard maintenance can generate plenty of material for compost, so consider setting up two compost systems: one for hot compost and the other for cold compost.

COVER CROPS

In addition to compost, cover crops keep soil fertile, prevent erosion, and maintain tilth, the term that describes soil that has a good texture and small pockets for air and water. These are essential for drainage and root development, giving soil far more than simply an application of fertilizer. Cover crops can be matched for the exact type of nutrition each soil needs and are highly effective for increasing soil fertility and pest management, as well as attracting beneficial pollinators.

Typically, a cover crop is sown in fall to grow over the winter, stabilizing soil and providing long-lasting nutrients through its roots. Summer cover crops can also be used, because they grow quickly and provide fertility and weed prevention in between the spring and fall planting. If your garden needs rejuvenation, sow several different types of cover crops throughout the year, continually turning the green foliage back into the soil. What to choose will vary depending on the time of year, the climate, and the type of garden. Here is a quick look at some of the most familiar cover crops.

ANNUAL RYEGRASS

One of the most effective cover crops, annual ryegrass forms a dense, shallow root system with long green, grassy leaves. A stand of ryegrass provides erosion control in summer or winter while also suppressing weeds. Sow seeds and allow plants to grow into a green patch, but don't let the plants go to seed. In cooler areas annual ryegrass will naturally die back with a hard frost. When ready to get the garden planted for your edible crops, turn the plants with a garden fork, digging up the roots and allowing the foliage to be incorporated back into the soil. Wait two weeks before sowing an edible crop.

BUCKWHEAT

A quick-growing annual, buckwheat is useful for weed suppression and typically sown in between crops in midsummer. Broadcast seeds for buckwheat during hot weather in midsummer and keep it watered until it germinates, and soon it will transform into grassy green shoots topped by white flowers that are a magnet for bees. Shortly after it flowers, mow with a scythe and turn the greens back into the soil. Wait two weeks before sowing an edible crop.

FIELD PEAS

Often planted in spring, field peas add organic matter and nitrogen to soil through their legume roots. Sow seeds in spring or in late fall, and allow plants to establish, flower, and remain in place as long as possible, before mowing the crop and turning.

OATS

A lovely ornamental plant that is welcome in a flower or food garden, oats are often sown along with field peas in spring as an effective cover crop. Frost sensitive, oats will not survive a cold winter yet will become an excellent ground cover to prevent weeds and erosion during warmer months. When left to mature, the seed heads nod gently in the wind and can be harvested for decorative flower arrangements.

PERENNIAL RYEGRASS

Often sown in the fall to control soil erosion during winter, perennial ryegrass germinates in cool soil and tolerates heavy clay, making it particularly adaptable to different geographic regions and soil types. Perennial ryegrass develops a thicker root system but with the same grassy top growth as its annual counterpart. Yet since it is a perennial, it will not die back during winter and can be harder to remove once established. Similarly to annual ryegrass, when you're ready to remove it, use a garden fork to turn the roots over and shake out the soil. Leave the plants lying on the ground to dry in place before reintroducing them into the soil. Wait two weeks before sowing an edible crop.

RED CLOVER

Red clover sweetens acidic soil and supports ladybugs, lacewings, and hoverfly larvae, which all feast on destructive aphids. Everyone should have a patch of red clover somewhere in their landscape, either sown into the lawn or in a garden bed in between to suppress weeds and sweeten the soil. Clover produces a thick web of roots and leaves and is sometimes planted in paths as a long-term perennial crop to suppress weeds.

7

STAY ORGANIZED

GARDEN SHEDS AND TOOLS

MULTIPLE OUTBUILDINGS WERE ONCE A standard part of creating a homestead, each with a specific purpose especially useful to farm living: a barn for animals, a blacksmithing shed for welding, and a root cellar for overwintering vegetables. Like a good pantry, a garden shed is best when it is large enough to keep everything you will use in the garden yet small enough to stay neatly organized and easily accessible.

Garden sheds are often left out of most garden plans, but they are an essential element that can't be overlooked. I use mine as both a potting bench and a place to sow seeds, transplant, and organize plant tags and stakes. Since it is dark and dry, I also use it to dry garlic and herbs and to hang dahlia tubers and other bulbs until they're ready to store for the winter.

HEIRLOOM TOOLS

Most garden tools have improved over time; on the other hand, some perfectly useful items have gone out of fashion and are difficult to find. For authenticity, seek out these tools to add to your collection.

DIBBER (OR DIBBLE)	A garden dibber is a pointed wooden stick used for making holes in the ground to place seedlings or bulbs. The first recorded dibber was used in Roman times: one man would walk along a row and mark holes, while another man would follow, planting seeds and covering them.
CLOCHE	This glass cover shaped like a dome is used to protect plants during cool weather. During the 1600s, they were handblown and fragile. In Colonial Williamsburg, they were used to protect cabbage, artichokes, cardoons, and endives during the cool winter months and removed in early spring.
HOT BED	This unique garden bed is used inside a cold frame or greenhouse for the purpose of nurturing tender crops along in early spring. It is heated with a bottom layer of dung or compost that naturally raises the temperature of the soil when it heats up.
STICKS OR WATTLE	In medieval Europe, sticks or osiers were collected from willows, hazels, alders, and other types of trees and used to form lattices, create domes, and support vines. They are not your typical sticks picked up off the ground; rather they are grown on specific trees selected just for this purpose. Few items were as useful to a gardener as a good supply of long, slender, supple sticks that looked stunning in a garden, especially as a wattle fence.

WHEEL-BARROW	Gardeners everywhere still rely on the wheelbarrow. During the Colonial Williamsburg era, wheelbarrows were made from wood with wooden wheels and sides; these were heavy-duty carts that could travel between orchard and field. The shape and use are much the same today, yet our modern wheelbarrows are surely an improved version.
WATERING CAN	The first watering can was most likely a dried and carved gourd. When the first tin can appeared in 1692, it was called a watering pot, and instead of a spout, it had holes in the bottom. Early antique cans are made from copper, iron, brass, and zinc, and the shape of the handles and the length of the spouts can date its history.
GARDEN FORK	Wooden tines prevailed until blacksmiths in Colonial Williamsburg introduced forged tines and attached them to wooden handles—still relatively frail given what a garden fork has to accomplish when digging into soil.
ROCK BOAT	This wooden platform has been used for centuries to clear heavy stones and tree stumps from a field. Originally pulled behind a team of oxen, rock boats are still used today but more often are attached to tractors instead of animals.

FRAMEWORK

STRUCTURES

IT'S TIME TO GO BEYOND the nuts and bolts of basic gardening techniques to explore ways that you can make your garden more than a healthy, thriving place to grow food and flowers. This involves adding elements that can both give the garden character and also add an element of surprise and whimsy.

THE GATE

Your heirloom garden starts at the gate. A unique gate can suggest the style or design of the garden beyond it. Maybe it's a simple wooden frame, a captivating arbor smothered with climbing roses, or an antique iron fence. Find something that accentuates this important transition between the lawn and the garden in a way that fits into the landscape. A gate creates a barrier but also a visual cue that will set the tone for the experience of entering the garden. Add a bell or a chime to ring before entering, as a reminder to take a deep breath and be present.

TRELLIS

We often think of vegetables as ground-hugging plants, yet many vegetables also love to grow vertically. Construct a trellis in the vegetable garden, and the height will instantly add a dramatic statement. This can easily be done by harnessing together a simple tripod of bamboo poles, or by installing an antique trellis you found at a yard sale. By adding a trellis you will add garden flair to an otherwise flat landscape. Plan to grow runner beans, gourds, cherry tomatoes, and decorative cucumbers that will weave together, giving the garden character and personality. Adorn a corner bench with fragrant vines, braiding in a fragrant moonflower that blooms in the evening. A range of plants can climb and ramble on a variety of vertical elements or even a stand-alone ornamental sculpture that twirls in the wind.

FOCAL POINT

Because focal points are what your eyes see first, professional gardeners frequently use them in a flower border to create visual order and balance. This concept is seen often in sweeping ornamental borders, yet it can easily be borrowed for the edible garden design, too, giving it personal style and dimension.

A focal point will catch your eye and draw you into the garden, capturing your attention. It might be as simple as a bench at the far end of the garden pathway, a classic obelisk placed in the center, or a large rock that makes a statement. Focal points can change from year to year, adding a bright spot of

color from a tall stand of smoldering orange and yellow sunflowers one year, then a trellis overflowing with deep blue morning glories the next.

THE FENCE

When I was in art school, we were not allowed to say a painting was complete unless it had a picture frame around it. The frame could be simple, like an unpainted wood panel, or more distinctive and painted a color to resonate with the painting. I have always thought of fences in the same way: as framing something beautiful. Instead of building a tall intimidating fence that wraps itself around the garden to keep out wildlife, consider instead how the fence can work in your favor. It is an enclosure, after all, that brings together a space, much like a room that you enter. Consider all the options for your fence, and take into account the beauty and aesthetics it will offer to your lovely heirloom garden.

9

PERSONALITY

STYLE

AN HEIRLOOM GARDEN MAY TAKE your senses back to an era when the flowers were fragrant and the flavors exquisite, yet also to when gardening was valued as an activity that would bring peace and tranquility to one's life. Adding personality to the garden can start with something as simple as a garden bench or a piece of art that makes you smile. Start with just a few elements and keep adding more as you find new ways to have more fun in your garden, turning it into a place that can provide nurturing and personal expression.

GARDEN BENCH

A bench in the garden does not guarantee that a gardener will sit still for a moment, but it does provide an opportunity, as well as a welcome reminder, to take a moment in your day to rest and enjoy the garden you have created. You may not find time during the day to sit on a bench, yet it can play a large part in your garden design. Perhaps after the sun has gone down and the garden tools are put away, the bench offers a place to reflect on the day. Sit and listen to the night noises and gaze at the stars. The garden bench can serve as a focal point as well as a place to sit, so it is important to find one that is both comfortable and fits your garden style. Don't settle for just any old bench; take time to find a bench that is made of a durable, weather-resistant wood that will last for many years. I have two benches in my garden, each facing the opposite direction to give me a full 360-degree perspective. Made of cedar, they are hitting their third decade and have developed a lovely heirloom patina of lichen, which only enhances their charm. Think long-term when selecting a bench: how would you like it to age in place in your garden? Move it around until you find that sweet spot—the place where you want to sit often with your tea in the morning or your glass of wine at night. A bench is one of the best investments you can make for the present moment and for the future.

GARDEN ART

I happen to love art in the garden. Gardens produce memories—of the food and the flowers but also of those things we place in the garden that remind us to smile and relax. Whether you love to scout antiques stores for ancient treasures or follow the latest trend on colors to paint the patio furniture, adding art to the garden is bringing your personality to the garden—which can be whimsical or artful, anything to make you and others feel good.

What I place in my garden is usually something sentimental or treasured, but I have noticed that there is a thin line between garden art and junk—no doubt a matter of personal taste. For some people the element might be a stone sculpture handed down from a grandmother, yet for me it is a collection of stone frogs and toads. I've turned my obsession into a treasure hunt, and when friends come over with young children, I hide all of these amphibians, then set the young ones off to find them. As they go in search of hidden treasures, they will nibble strawberries and cherry tomatoes along the way or brush against the mint, adding to their sensory experiences—and their memory of my garden.

Art in the garden can be the focal point, or it may be a collection of small items or a handcrafted iron trellis to hold up the runner beans. It brings everything together in a way that reflects aesthetics and style and adds to the feeling of comfort and sanctuary.

FROM SEED TO SEED

IN THE SPRING, when the days are longer and the garden is moving into full swing, I am often in that glass-half-full kind of mood. Like a well-synchronized orchestra, the asparagus spears emerge in beat with the rosy knobs of rhubarb, and that dizzy feeling comes into my head. I eagerly rip open another seed packet, mark the row in soft soil with a trowel, and gently press seeds into the furrow. It is a familiar spring ritual that taps into that happy place where my worries and the world melt away. Once the tiny green tips of arugula and lettuce press through the soil and peas wrap tendrils up the trellis, I'm gone.

All gardeners are stewards of the land. When we turn over soil for the first time in the spring, we are forming a partnership with the earth. Pushing a seed in the ground, then stepping back and waiting for it to grow into a plant that eventually provides nourishment is, well, just nothing short of a miracle. Seeds are life-giving, providing the basis for food, clothing, and shelter, yet they also form the basis for almost everything we fight against when we attempt to gain control of our landscape—when we battle with invasive plants and weeds.

Yet few of us really know much about seeds or take the time to look at where they come from or how they are designed to grow—including me. Tired of the limited choices of common varieties that were available in the commercial seed catalogs, I found sources for European and American heirloom and open-pollinated seeds, which offer a wildly different experience from growing plants simply to eat.

As a cook, I also considered the other reason to grow heirlooms besides flavor and uniqueness: to preserve the diversity of plants that were slipping away as the availability of these seeds rapidly diminished. Recognizing the need to preserve the older varieties that were being lost at a rapid pace and the rising concern around genetically modified organisms (GMOs), the abundance of sterile (pollen-less) flowers, and ubiquitous hybrids that offer disease resistance and higher yields, I often was stuck between what's ordinary and commonly available in the nurseries and what is extraordinary, exceptional, and transcendent. We have lost over 85 percent of the plant world in the past century to extinction.

Fortunately, and in the nick of time, there are a growing number of smaller, farm-based seed catalogs cropping up in every state, intent on preserving treasured old varieties from each planting region. I encourage gardeners to support these catalogs published by people who are growing heirloom seeds that are adapted to climate and geography, contain stories of local yore, and are named after the places where they have grown, a person who saved the seed, or an attribute of the plant itself—once a way of life that is slowly returning to our gardens.

For the past twelve thousand years, gardeners and small-scale farmers have been the keepers of seeds and stewards of the land. Growing heirloom seeds is an opportunity to share a bit of history while conserving the unique heritage that comes from plants. When we respect all aspects of growing food, from nurturing the soil to sowing seeds, breeding and raising plants for harvest, then allowing seedpods to naturally develop into another generation of seeds, we are guardians of this valuable tradition.

Seed catalogs are a fairly recent business model, and most rely on a system of reselling seeds each year—yet open-pollinated seeds can be saved year after year, and traded hand to hand. The currency of a seed shared with another gardener is a gift of reciprocity that belongs to everyone. I invite you to step into your new heirloom garden to grow food and flowers while you also learn to start and save your own seeds.

SEED SELECTION

The best part of growing an heirloom garden is the wide range of vegetables, fruits, flowers, and herbs that you can grow—all from seed! Seed catalogs are designed to charm the gardener with color photographs, but instead of being seduced by the pictures, learn to read the text. Start early, but don't order until you have pored through all the catalogs, dog-eared the pages, and crafted notes on the varieties that you want.

Take your time to fully explore all the options available—both online and in print. Look to local and regional companies for seeds that might be specifically adapted to your climate. Take a closer look at the whole system of how seeds arrive in your mailbox, and support the local smaller growers who understand that the future of our food supply depends on seeds.

In the catalog or on the website, look for helpful information, such as tips for sowing indoors, days to maturity, and descriptions of height and sun requirements. Does it mention flavor or what to pair with it in the garden or in the kitchen? Make a wish list that includes "tried and true" and "new and different" to keep learning and pushing the boundaries of what you can grow.

Once your seeds arrive, set up a planting chart based on whether the seeds will be started indoors or planted directly in the garden. Long-season crops such as onions, tomatoes, and peppers are typically started indoors six to eight weeks before the frost-free date; squash, cucumbers, and many flowers need to be planted four weeks before this date. Lettuce, peas, chard, and other cool-weather crops can be sown directly in the garden as soon as the soil is prepared, while frost-sensitive plants must wait until after the frost-free date.

SOWING SEEDS INDOORS

Seeding trays come in a range of sizes and materials, such as plastic containers or peat pots. You can make your own seed tubes by rolling newspapers into a small pot or using a milk carton. Create a system that works easily for you, given your space. Start by filling a seedling tray or small pot with potting soil. Gently moisten the soil and press the seeds into the soil to a depth of one and a half times the size of the seed. Cover the seeds with a dusting of loose potting soil or vermiculite, which is a lightweight mineral often used in the garden industry. Gently press the seeds to make contact with the moist soil, which will trigger a message to the seed to let the embryo inside release and start to grow. Keep the soil moist and warm, and once the seeds germinate and green leaves emerge, move the seedlings into a full-sun location or place them under grow lights.

Germination varies between seed varieties and temperatures, yet it typically takes between three and ten days for tiny green shoots to appear. Once the second true set of leaves appears, usually after several weeks of nurturing the seedling, and a good root system is established, the plants are ready to transplant into the garden.

ANNUALS, PERENNIALS, BIENNIALS, AND ROOTSTOCK

Every heirloom garden starts off with a wish list of plants. In this book's twelve designs, you will find varieties that are largely based on ones that I have successfully grown in my Vermont garden, but you will most likely need to adapt and swap out varieties to match your own growing location. Southern gardeners can't grow the same plants we can grow in cool northern or northwestern gardens. Success requires you to seek out seeds and plants that adapt to your seasonal climate and geography.

There are hundreds of edibles that are available to the heirloom gardener, but I strongly encourage you to limit what you grow to the space that you have and to the varieties that can't commonly be found in the local markets. After all, why would you grow the same tomatoes, lettuce, and carrots that are commonly available in stores when you can grow the best-tasting varieties that are available from your own garden? Look for the unusual, hard-to-find crops that you can experience only if you grow them yourself.

In an heirloom garden, you may choose to grow a range of annuals, biennials, and perennials—and the new gardener may need to learn the language. Here's a short primer to help you get started.

ANNUALS

Annuals are quick to progress from seed to blossom to seed, and a single plant can keep regenerating itself through this cycle. Annual plants live a single season, dying back in the fall or winter when the temperatures drop below freezing. It is best to keep the seed heads from forming in order to force the plant to continue to grow and to produce more leaves and flowers. Some plants, such as zinnias, are described as "cut and come again": the more you cut, the larger the blossoms and the longer the stems, so it helps to keep trimming them back all summer. At the end of the season, allow them to go to seed to save for future garden years.

PERENNIALS

Perennials are plants that will come back each year, going dormant when the temperatures drop and disappearing back into the earth. They will return in the spring and generate new foliage during the growing season. They are generally frost hardy, but when buying perennials, know your garden zone as established by the US Department of Agriculture (USDA) to be sure the plants will survive your area's average winter temperatures. Gardeners often cut back the seedpods and stems at the end of the season, but to establish a diverse and eco-friendly environment, it is best to leave spent foliage for caterpillars to overwinter and seedpods for the birds. Perennial edibles include some herbs, asparagus, rhubarb, horseradish, berries, and nuts—all are ornamental and thrive under the right conditions.

BIENNIALS

This group of plants starts as a seed and takes two years to grow into a mature plant, bloom, and then disappear. If the plant is left to go to seed in the wild, it will sow seeds that will then regrow, often where the former plant once existed. Many of the vegetable crops that are grown for seed are biennials, especially the cabbage or brassica family, although we grow them as annuals in the garden. If you plan to grow the plants for saving seed, it's best to dig up the plants and store them in cool conditions until spring, when they are replanted and a seed head develops in the center of the plant.

ROOTSTOCK

Some plants, such as perennial flowers, shrubs, fruits, and trees, are best started from a cutting derived from the original parent plant. This is a method used mostly by nurseries and experienced gardeners to generate more plants quickly as well as produce specimens that more accurately match the original DNA of the plant. Heritage orchards rely on this system for splicing together rootstock of older varieties with more disease-resistant stock to create a hardier heritage breed.

DIRECT SOWING IN THE GARDEN

Prepare your garden soil by gently turning over the soil with a garden fork, adding compost, and removing all the stones and weeds. Rake it smooth and mark the planting rows by stretching twine between two sticks to form a straight line, and then make a furrow with a dibber or stick. Sprinkle the seeds into the row, cover with soil, and press gently. Lightly water the soil with the spray nozzle on a hose or with a watering can, and wait. Similarly to starting seeds indoors, it will typically take between three and ten days for green sprouts to appear. If necessary, thin the rows to allow each plant enough room to grow to full size. Be sure to give each plant plenty of room; as with people, overcrowding can lead to stress and disease.

TRANSPLANTING INTO THE GARDEN

Even though most plants love the sun, it is best to wait until an overcast or slightly rainy day to transplant. Avoid the hot midday sun, which will stress the plants' systems and make their leaves and stems wither; if this is the only option, use a shade cloth to protect the seedlings until they are well established. Mark the garden with a dibber or the back of a hoe, allowing space between rows, then dig a shallow hole with a trowel and gently place the plant in the hole. Add water mixed with a water-soluble high-phosphorus fertilizer such as Neptune's Harvest, which is a fish emulsion that gives the roots a boost. Finally, backfill the hole with soil, tamp lightly, and water again.

STAYING WEED-FREE

Your garden will involve many steps along the way, yet cultivating the soil throughout the summer to keep it weed-free is one of the most important tasks. Pulling weeds by hand, making sure the roots come up with the leaves, is the most effective option. Gently run a hoe along the rows between the plants to dislodge weed seedlings, and the daily or weekly regimen of pulling weeds should minimize the weeds that naturally populate in any open soil. Layering plants to take up as much space as possible and staging them based on height, as well as sowing cover crops during times that the garden is not planted, are effective in covering any open areas that will be susceptible to weed seeds.

SEED SAVING

Inside the hard coat of a seed is a fragile embryo that will become the next generation of a cherished variety. Some seeds can last for years, while others have shorter life spans. Some seeds are easy to grow and save, while others require more skill. While you may be able to save seeds on a small scale, there are some crops that require a bit more know-how. Consult the true seed experts who have written detailed books about all aspects of seed-saving techniques and can provide more in-depth resources.

How you store your seeds, whether homegrown, handed down, or bought, impacts the viability and longevity of the seed, no matter the variety. Most seed catalogs send their seeds in a paper envelope, which allows the seed to breathe and is lightweight for shipping, but it is not ideal for long-term storage. When your seeds arrive, put them in a cool, dry location, away from the sun, so moisture and humidity will not hinder germination.

SHORT-TERM STORAGE

If you are storing seeds for the following year's garden, it is safe to save them in paper envelopes, cloth bags, or tin boxes. These natural materials allow air to flow, adjusting for any respiration that may occur during storage. Be sure everything is properly marked with a label, both inside and outside the container, including date, varietal name, and where it was grown. Store seed envelopes upright in a seed box, grouped by the type: vegetable, flower, and herb. For extra protection against mice, use a glass jar with a lid. (One gardener I know found a cache of seeds in a mouse nest; each type of seed was divided into piles by type. Takes an organized mouse!)

LONG-TERM STORAGE

If you plan to keep your seeds for a long time, consider storing them in a glass jar with a tight-fitting lid and placing it in the freezer. Again, be sure everything is properly marked with labels, both inside and outside the container, including date, varietal name, and where it was grown. When seeds are stored in a sealed container, the moisture content will remain relatively stable regardless of the surrounding environment. Once the lid is opened, the seeds will draw in moisture from the air, and their viability will begin to degrade. Make it quick, and remove the seeds that you plan to use for that season, seal the jar, and return it to the freezer.

HEIRLOOM GARDEN
DESIGNS

WHY AN HEIRLOOM GARDEN?

The words *heirloom garden* might bring to mind the era when a young bride and groom would plant their first garden with seeds and fruit grafts given to them as wedding gifts by relatives. Proud to carry on the legacy of their ancestors, the couple would nurture and tend a young Cox's Orange Pippin apple tree and greengage plum tree as a pledge to their future. Together, they would harvest fat Scarlet Keeper carrots, layering them in the root cellar along with Blue Hubbard squash and Gilfeather turnip, leaving a few plants in the ground to allow them to go to seed. Gardening from seed to seed was a promise that there would be both food for the winter and seeds for another growing season the following year.

An heirloom, as defined by the dictionary, can be either a valuable object that has belonged to a family for several generations or a plant or breed of animal that is not associated with large-scale commercial agriculture. The term originated in England, combining the two words *heir* ("inheritance") and *loom* ("tool") as a way of passing along property without a written document or legal settlement. Heirloom gardens were simply the way people gardened; they were a place to grow food when life itself was totally dependent on the plant world in a way that our modern culture no longer recognizes.

Seed saving was a necessity but also a link to the past. Some of the heirloom seeds that we grow today were brought to the United States by immigrants who smuggled seeds inside the linings of coats, suitcases, and hatbands, or sewn into the hems of dresses. Handed down from family to family, seeds were something small they could bring to connect them to their homeland. All heirloom seeds are open-pollinated, which means that if you save the seeds, the resulting plant from that seed will be similar to the original parent plants. It's the way of continuing the cycle of life and a guarantee that there will be another garden the following season.

In this design chapter, I've taken classic design elements and merged history and nostalgia to create a New Heirloom Garden. You'll find twelve designs for heirloom kitchen gardens inspired in part by nostalgia, based on real places and people. Heirloom seed experts help to fill in the gaps, sharing the reasons they grow heirlooms and favorites.

1

THE "ARK OF TASTE" GARDEN

ENDANGERED SPECIES

DESIGN NOTES

Explore this rich international heritage garden based on varieties from ancient civilizations, selected by Slow Food USA as endangered species. In this garden you will find a diverse collection of heirloom and open-pollinated varieties that are no longer grown in modern large-scale agriculture.

INSPIRATION

Slow Food is a nonprofit organization dedicated to preserving heritage foods from around the world. In 1996 more than 3,500 products from over 50 countries (including 200 from the United States) were identified as being endangered and facing extinction. The carefully selected list of foods known as the Ark of Taste includes livestock breeds and artisan foods such as sausages, bread, honey, and cheeses and other dairy products, as well as unique regional cultivars of vegetables, fruits, and herbs grown from heirloom seeds or rootstock.

This garden represents a small tasting sampler and only suggests a sliver of options available through the Ark of Taste master list. Since most of these seeds are not readily available through mainstream seed catalogs, your challenge is to track them down through seed-saver exchanges, niche seed catalogs, and seed libraries, or to find substitutes that are similar in nature. By learning more about these endangered varieties and adding them to the diversity of your own garden, you are participating in a worldwide effort to save these seeds (and plants) from extinction and preserve culinary history.

THE "ARK OF TASTE" GARDEN

DESIGN WISDOM
TIPS FOR GROWING

MULTIPLE GARDEN BEDS

Make the most of the series of small beds and maze of paths to grow a large range of diverse varieties in a compact area.

LET THERE BE SEEDS

It's easier than you think to save seeds for most vegetables, yet it often means not harvesting the crops at prime time. Establish some beds for fresh eating and others for seed saving. Most seeds need plenty of space in order to stay pure and not cross-pollinate.

FIND THE BALANCE

A shady corner bench covered with a climbing vine creates a place where, hopefully, you will find time to sit, relax, inhale, and fully enjoy your garden.

UNDERSTORY PLANTING

By grouping tall, medium, and short plants together in a single bed, you can fit more into the space. Plant tall artichokes with an understory of purple basil and ground-hugging nasturtiums. Group plants by height as well as by how they will grow together in a unified design.

MAKE AN ENTRANCE

Placing the entrance to the garden at the corner creates a dramatic way to enter the garden. Cover an arbor with an aromatic honeysuckle or wisteria vine or a more practical edible vining plant like purple Trionfo Violetto pole bean.

GROW LOCAL

Seek out local indigenous heirlooms that will match your geographical heritage. If you can't grow a succulent salad green because you live in the Southwest, substitute a more rugged Mediterranean chicory that will succeed.

GLOBE-TROTTING

When traveling, visit farmers' markets and farms to learn more about local cuisine and cultures. If possible (and legal), bring back seeds for your own garden.

BE BOLD

Slow Food USA is always on the lookout for new additions to preserve and add to its Ark of Taste inventory. Join forces with them to find something unusual for the worldwide list.

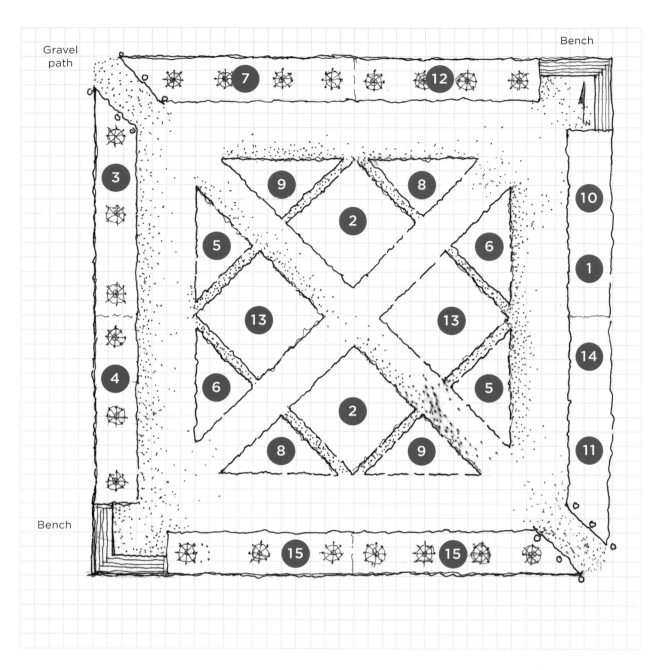

Gravel path

Bench

Bench

PLANT KEY

☐ = 1 square foot

1. **AMARANTH:** Hopi Red Dye
2. **ARTICHOKE:** Sant'Erasamo or Violet de Provence
3. **BEAN:** Hidatsa Red shelling bean
4. **BEET:** Early Blood Turnip-Rooted
5. **CHICORY:** Radicchio Variegata di Castelfranco
6. **CLAYTONIA:** Miner's lettuce
7. **CUCUMBER:** West Indian Burr gherkin
8. **FLOWER:** (*Papaver somniferum*) Hungarian Blue Breadseed

9. **FLOWER:** Anise hyssop
10. **FLOWER:** (*Tithonia rotundifolia*) Mexican sunflower
11. **GARLIC:** Nubia Red or Spanish Roja
12. **HUSK GROUND-CHERRY:** Aunt Molly's
13. **LETTUCE:** Forellenschluss
14. **ONION:** I'Itoi or Red Creole
15. **TOMATO:** Cherokee Purple

SEED TALK

HEIRLOOM SEED SAVER WILL BONSALL

"Genetic diversity is the hedge between us and global famine," writes Will Bonsall, author of *Will Bonsall's Essential Guide to Radical, Self-Reliant Gardening* and founder of the Scatterseed Project. In the far reaches of the western Maine mountains, Bonsall collects, maintains, and distributes plants and seeds, many of them rare or endangered. He's been featured in the documentary *Seed: The Untold Story* and is best known for his work in promoting the importance of preserving diversity.

"*Extinction* is a term we often hear attributed to wild things but not to agriculture," says Bonsall, in a phone interview. He says that 94 percent of vegetable seed varieties were lost during the twentieth century, as global agriculture became more consolidated and food production moved away from local farms and backyard gardens, resulting in vanishing heritage varieties.

How did you become a seed saver?

I am an avid gardener and started saving seeds, not to preserve diversity like other seed savers, but to save money. I am into self-sufficiency, and it did not make sense to order the same seeds from seed catalogs if I could grow my own. But I learned from an old Yankee farmer who lived down the road and maintained a shelling type of pole bean, a variety I had never seen or tasted. I named the bean Orlando after him and grew out the seeds to make sure they continued.

He also had a weird-looking potato called a cow horn—an ugly purplish thing, shaped like a horn and scrawny, too—and a lima bean, which was not a true lima but a white runner bean that he got from another local fellow who got it in the Carolinas. These were the first seeds that turned me into a seed saver.

What is the Scatterseed Project?

The Scatterseed Project is based on not keeping too many eggs in the same basket. I want more people to be keeping their own seeds, so the forgotten foods are in circulation longer.

The word *germplasm* is the name of the genetic material preserved in seed banks but unavailable to the general public. Getting seeds out in the world is the opposite of holding them in a seed bank for preservation, and this is what my goal is. Not to feed the world, but to feed myself and let others feed themselves, too, by learning to save seeds.

What is your priority at Scatterseed Project?

I am not a seed bank or a seed catalog, but my goal is to maintain diversity in order to keep the seeds in circulation. Varieties remain viable if people are growing and eating them; otherwise seed catalogs take them off their list and they are gone. Since most home gardeners only need a small amount of seeds, I can supply them through Scatterseed, but I would not be able to handle a large order from a market grower.

Do you have favorites?

I don't put attention on the beans, tomatoes, peppers, and squash that most seed banks hold. Instead, I save seed for kohlrabi or parsnip or rutabaga, which are biennial and not as well known in this country because we don't have a tradition of saving the seeds.

The key is to grow all kinds of things in order to be as sustainable as possible. I grow my own grain—oats, barley, buckwheat, and soybeans—not because I have to but because I can. I am not the authority on anything, but I am curious, and the diversity is dazzling.

2

THE PARTERRE GARDEN

FOUR-SQUARE DESIGN

DESIGN NOTES

A parterre garden is a formal design that is enclosed and often set into a four-square pattern around a central axis. The design goes back centuries and is often paired with pruned hedges, stone walls, and espaliered trees. Parterre is ideal for the gardener who loves an orderly place to grow food, flowers, and fruits, yet also suits the organic gardener who rotates crops to keep healthy soil.

INSPIRATION

Above my drawing board is a postcard of a garden in Colonial Williamsburg depicting a classic four-square parterre, defined by boxwood, circular brick paths, two white benches, and an orderliness that reflects a simple design.

Visiting Colonial Williamsburg today, you will be greeted by gardeners who tend to ornamental four-square parterres next to homes. Each is surrounded by boxwood, decorated with espaliered fruit trees, and features beds fenced in by woven willow, or wattle.

Virginia soil is rich and fertile, yet of the five hundred colonists living at Jamestown in the fall of 1609, only sixty remained a few months later, and nearly everyone felt the "sharpe pricke of hunger." That first winter they nearly starved because their English seeds were not adapted to this new climate. Thankfully, the many tribes of the neighboring Powhatan Nation taught the colonists how to practice subsistence farming.

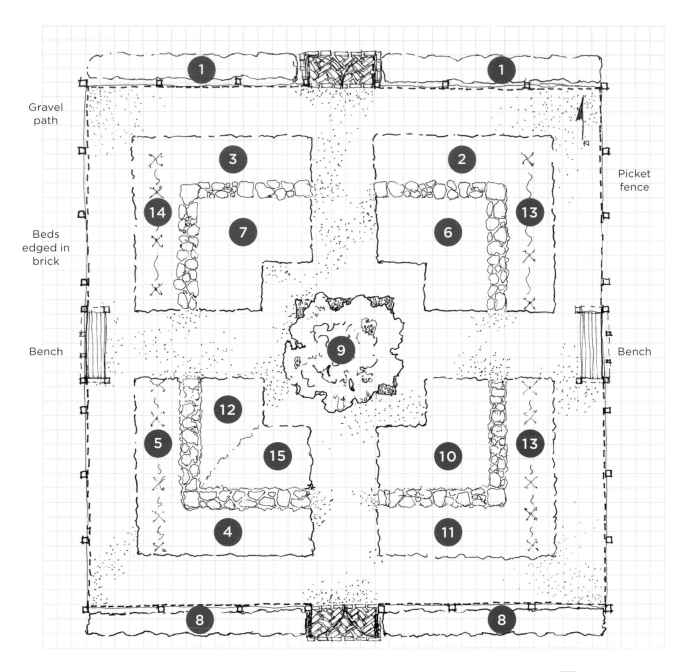

Gravel path

Picket fence

Beds edged in brick

Bench

Bench

PLANT KEY

☐ = 1 square foot

1. **ASPARAGUS:** Mary Washington or Martha Washington
2. **BROCCOLI:** Purple Sprouting
3. **CABBAGE:** Savoy
4. **CARDOON:** Gobbo di Nizzia or Bianca Avorio
5. **CHARD:** Fordhook Giant
6. **FLOWER:** Calendula Flashback
7. **FLOWER:** Nasturtium Empress of India
8. **FLOWER:** Pansy Bowles Black

9. **FRUIT:** Bosc Pear
10. **LETTUCE:** Tennis Ball and Spotted Aleppo
11. **MELON:** Jenny Lind
12. **ONION:** Welsh Bunching
13. **PEA:** Prince Albert or Green Arrow
14. **POLE BEAN:** Scarlet runner
15. **SALSIFY (AKA OYSTER ROOT):** Mammoth Sandwich Island

THE PARTERRE GARDEN

DESIGN WISDOM
TIPS FOR GROWING

MANURE POWER
Eighteenth-century gardeners were very particular about the manure they used for crops; each added high fertility to the soil. If you can find a local source for well-rotted manure to scratch into your garden soil, your plants will most likely thrive.

ACCEPT IMPERFECTION
Some of the pests we find in our gardens are modern interlopers and did not exist in eighteenth-century Virginia. But as was the case for our predecessors, learning to live with blemishes on our vegetables comes with the territory.

FORM FOLLOWS FUNCTION
Annuals and biennials produce seeds that are collected at the end of the season. If you choose to save the seeds, carefully dry and package them in a paper envelope, clearly marking it with the date and varietal information.

HIDE IN PLAIN SIGHT
A toolshed is useful for storage or potting. Besides garden tools, everything from clay pots to harvest baskets can be stored in a well-organized shed.

PLAY UP PERIOD PANACHE
Few things are more beautiful than terra-cotta or glass cloches to protect hardy plants during winter; a line of espaliered fruit trees; or crab-apple branches trimmed and used to support the peas. Keep it simple and natural.

KEEP IT WATERED
Consider us lucky that we no longer need to bring water from a well or cistern. Modern hoses and sprinklers offer a more efficient and time-saving way to satisfy thirsty plants. Consider another step toward water conservation with drip irrigation or soaker hoses to get the water directly to the roots of the plants.

SEASON EXTENDERS
Grow edibles year-round, or add a few weeks at the beginning and the end of the growing season by cultivating plants in a greenhouse or cold frame. Construct a simple tunnel with bamboo or bent branches that can form a structure over which you can drape a light cloth to protect tender plants from frost.

BE NATURAL
Feeding the soil with compost, manure, and cover crops is the organic way, yet it was once the only way before chemicals. Gardens attract a diversity of birds, caterpillars, snakes, and toads, and it's best to allow the natural ecosystem to flourish.

ADD A BENCH
For those moments of reflection and rest, a well-placed bench can be a focal point at the end of a long garden path, or it can be hidden behind leafy vines.

SEED TALK

HEIRLOOM ORCHARDIST EZEKIEL GOODBAND

If you've ever stood in an orchard at the peak of peach season, inhaling the scent of ripeness, you'll never buy supermarket fruit again. Scott Farm in Dummerston, Vermont, preserves heirloom apples, plums, and other fruits picked at the moment of perfection. To get there, you cross a covered bridge over the Connecticut River, turn through a village with a white church and town hall, and drive two miles on a dirt road through a national forest and past Rudyard Kipling's historic home, Naulakha.

Ezekiel Goodband has been growing heirloom apples for more than forty years; when I visited with him, he had been the orchardist at the Scott Farm for almost twenty years. (He's since moved on to Champlain Orchards, where he is busy grafting and still searching for nearly lost varieties.) Now owned and preserved by the Landmark Trust USA, Kipling's house, built in 1791 near the apple storage barn, originated as a tavern. "It was the local drinking hole for the community," explains Goodband. "Drinking fermented wild apple cider was safer than drinking water, and with plenty of wild apples around, it seemed the natural choice."

In 1903, the farm was taken over by the Holbrook family and run as a gentleman's dairy farm. "There is the creamery and cow barn," says Goodband, pointing downhill to a tall, naturally aged barn. "The floors are made of cork for the comfort of the cows' legs." Cork was also used as insulation in the coolers to keep fruit at the optimal temperature, just above freezing.

Over the decades, outbuildings proliferated, including a horse barn, a carpenter's shop, a mechanic's shop, and a sawmill, and what is now called Scott Farm soon became the largest employer in this remote Vermont valley. By the end of the 1800s, there were thousands of wild trees growing on the property, all harvested to press into cider. In 1911, the farm switched from dairy to apples, replacing the wild varieties with named cultivars such as Dutchess, Northern Spy, Macintosh, and Canadian strains that could withstand the cool temperatures of the valley. During the last half of the twentieth century, the orchard expanded, yet the price of apples was so low that the farm was not able to support the crop, and the trees suffered from lack of proper maintenance.

Enter Goodband, who arrived at the farm in 2001, when the price of apples was $4.15 per bushel, yet the price to produce them was $6.00. On his first visit, he walked the orchard, noticed the trees were mostly overgrown into a tangle of branches, and knew instinctively what needed to be done. He cut the trees below the branch line, spliced small branches, or scions, from heritage varieties into the open tree trunks of more vigorous trees, then stepped back. The young grafts gave way to productive trees that now bring this farm its excellent reputation.

The current crop of 130 heritage varieties grown at Scott Farm is far more limited than what might have grown in earlier years, yet it reflects Goodband's personal favorites: D'Arcy Spice and Blue Pearmain, which are crisp and sweet but not cloying like the well-known Honeycrisp. Choosing apples based on flavor is a priority, which most often means choosing older varieties that have a specific use—for either cooking, fresh eating, or storage to make cider during the winter months. Harvest begins in mid-August for the early varieties, which are often tart, yielding to sweeter ones, then the long-lasting storage types.

Goodband prefers not to use herbicides at Scott Farm, instead allowing the natural cycle of the birds and bugs to work in harmony. "I call it ecologically grown," says Goodband, who is deeply tanned from hours spent outdoors. He encourages birds to nest and mows infrequently to enhance biodiversity and create a stable ecosystem.

3

THE COLOR
WHEEL GARDEN

BEST
NUTRITIONAL
VARIETIES

DESIGN NOTES

Flavor and optimum health go hand in hand when growing a garden, yet knowing which varieties to choose for higher antioxidant qualities can influence what you plant. Science has shown that vegetables and fruits in vibrant colors—deep purple, blue, orange, and red—contain more phytonutrients, flavonoids, resveratrol, and anthocyanins than those in paler colors. Plant openhearted lettuces, bitter chicories, purple tomatoes, and red onions to change up your ordinary garden plan.

INSPIRATION

Plant breeding, both by natural selection and in a lab, has been dictating what we eat for thousands of years. What's left behind for us to eat, grow, or buy in a supermarket is a narrow selection compared to the genetic heritage that every edible plant contains. While not all of us can or want to be foragers, we can choose to plant our gardens with species that closely resemble the earliest cultivars to experience the rich flavors, deep colors, and healthier selections that were once plentiful in the wild.

Stop pulling those weeds and instead cultivate them: purslane, dandelion, and chickweed are all ancient greens that grow readily in our gardens, with far more vitamin E than cultivated spinach, four times more omega-3 fatty acids than lettuce, and seven times more beta-carotene than carrots, plus high levels of iron and calcium. Blue potatoes, originally discovered in the Andes, contain more minerals and nutrients than an Idaho spud. Grow tiny Red Currant tomatoes, which may make your mouth pucker, yet the diminutive size and deep color are closer to those of their native cousins than those of large, modern, sweet beefsteaks.

THE COLOR WHEEL GARDEN

DESIGN WISDOM

TIPS FOR GROWING

PLANT APPRECIATION	Grow richly hued fruits and vegetables that contain anthocyanins. Science suggests that choosing purple, blue, and orange vegetables and fruits is better for our health, yet these varieties make up only 3 percent of the average American's diet.
VARIATIONS ON THE THEME	Plan to stagger height and color throughout the garden by grouping plants based on size and days to maturity. Grow nasturtiums under broccoli or cabbage next to onions, making the most of the high-to-low areas of the garden.
HIGH IMPACT	Mass plantings are robust and make the garden easier to maintain by concentrating plants that require similar amounts of sun or shade, water, and fertilizer together. It also makes them easier to harvest at the end of the season.
CURVES AHEAD	Build waves of color into the design and give your garden a more elegant feel by planting with curves and arcs. It takes a little advance planning on paper first, then staking out the garden, but once the seedlings start coming up and the color builds, you'll be delighted.
SOLAR FLAIR	Sprinkle solar-powered night-lights around the garden, on steps, at the entrance, or hanging from a nearby tree. It'll be an invitation to spend time outside past dark, when you can sit and listen to the night noises.
MIX IT UP	Pollinators love diversity, so plant a range of their favorites in large blocks to give them a place to lay eggs and to support larvae to keep your garden naturally healthy and pest-free.
TAKE IT DOWN	Color is welcome in a garden, yet sometimes too many colors can clash. If the colors are too hot, weave together neutral colors, such as gray foliage plants like artemisia or culinary sage, or pure white flowers, to soften the tone.

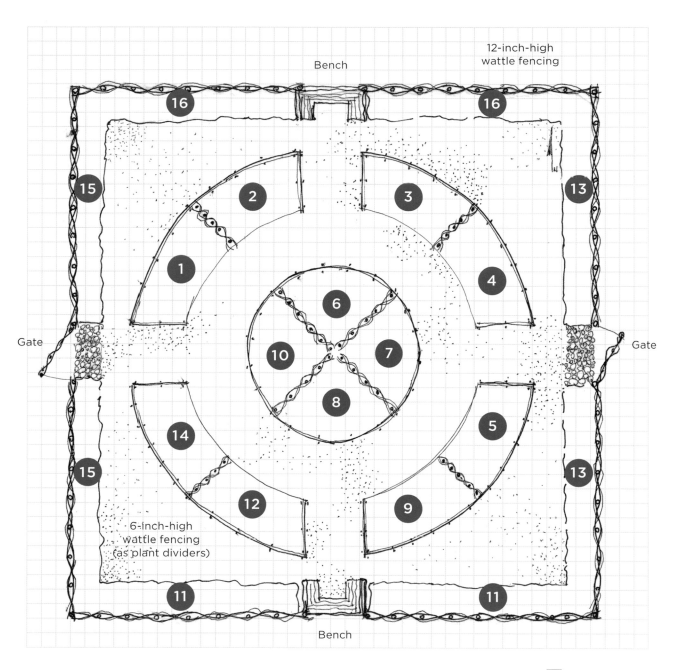

Bench

12-inch-high
wattle fencing

Gate

Gate

6-inch-high
wattle fencing
(as plant dividers)

Bench

PLANT KEY

☐ = 1 square foot

1. **ALLIUM:** Frog's Leg or Zebrune shallot
2. **BEET:** Chioggia
3. **BRUSSELS SPROUT:** Rubine
4. **CARROT:** Cosmic Purple
5. **COLLARDS:** Champion or Vates
6. **FLOWER:** Nasturtium Vesuvius
7. **HERB:** French tarragon
8. **HERB:** Tricolor sage

9. **LETTUCE:** Merlot
10. **MUSTARD:** Purple Osaka
11. **PEA:** Snow Peas Carouby de Maussane
12. **PEPPER:** Long Red Cayenne
13. **POTATO:** Purple Peruvian
14. **SPINACH:** Bloomsdale Long Standing
15. **SUNLOWERS:** Mixed colors
16. **TOMATO:** Red Currant

4

THE PERMACULTURE GARDEN

SUSTAINABLE LANDSCAPE DESIGN

DESIGN NOTES

Sometimes the beauty in our gardens is not really about the design but the glorious ways that nature exists all on its own to form a partnership among the plants, people, and landscape. In this heirloom garden that is a little bit wild, growing edibles alongside fruit and nut trees is a long-term investment, and less disruptive to the natural ecosystem.

INSPIRATION

A permaculture design plan is as individual as the gardener. Learning more about your specific microclimate, and existing native species that support wildlife habits, will involve taking time to observe before you begin to clear the land to make way for a garden. Once the garden is established, it is key to maintain a bit of wildness in order to invite pollinators to burrow into hollow plant stems and birds to eat seeds and berries.

The basic premise of a permaculture garden is to plant a wide range of food and flora, trees, shrubs, tubers, and vines that stimulate one another's growth. The result is productivity and a balanced ecosystem. It begins by first assessing the existing landscape—looking at patterns of sun, shade, and the geology under the soil—then moves to designing a long-term plan for the landscape. Permaculture is inclusive and supportive of a diverse selection of plants that ultimately nourishes a whole ecosystem; if a plant does not work in a certain area, move it to another.

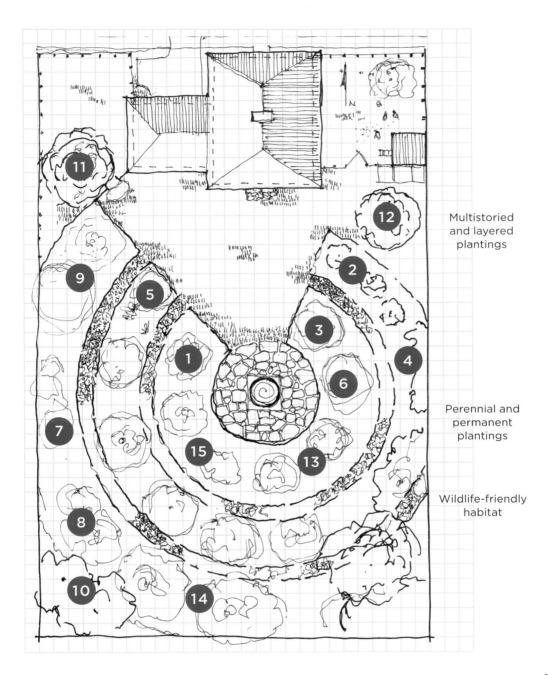

Multistoried
and layered
plantings

Perennial and
permanent
plantings

Wildlife-friendly
habitat

PLANT KEY

$\square$ = 5 square feet

1. **ALPINE STRAWBERRY:** Mignonette
2. **BLUEBERRY:** Highbush (northern or southern)
3. **BORAGE:** (*Borago officinalis*)
4. **ELDERBERRY:** (*Sambucus nigra*) European elderberry
5. **GREENS:** Malabar spinach
6. **HERB:** Pineapple sage
7. **HORSERADISH**
8. **JERUSALEM ARTICHOKE:** Beaver Valley Purple

9. **NUT TREE:** Hazelnut
10. **PEAR:** Bartlett
11. **PERSIMMON:** Saijo
12. **PLUM:** Green Gage and Shiro
13. **RHUBARB:** Victoria
14. **ROSE:** Rugosa rose
15. **THYME:** Old English

THE PERMACULTURE GARDEN

DESIGN WISDOM
TIPS FOR GROWING

LESS IS MORE

Go for diversity rather than massing with a single variety. Plant a wide range of different trees, fruits, and nuts for an array of species that support a variety of habitats for nature and food production.

FOCUS ON EDIBLE PERENNIALS

Edible perennial plants come back each year. Think rhubarb and asparagus, horseradish and berries. This will save you money and the effort to replant.

KEEP A JOURNAL

A garden journal is one way to track how much the landscape changes from year to year. Writing only a few lines each day to note activities, weather, or what's in bud makes it fun to look back and note progress.

RECYCLED MATERIALS

Seek out old brick, stone, or recycled lumber that can be salvaged and renovated to upcycle in your garden. Besides rescuing materials from the landfill, build compost piles from pallets, and paths from old logs sliced into pavers.

PASSIVE SOLAR

Make the most of a south-facing exposure to capture the warmth of the sun by employing warming stone or brick to reflect heat back into the garden. Go a step further by installing solar panels to heat a greenhouse, or charge dim lights for night strolling in the garden.

ENCOURAGE ALL INSECTS

The truth is that with good bugs, you also need to have bad bugs, because they rely on each other to exist. Before killing a bug, look it up to see what it does and how it fits into the cycle of the insect kingdom.

WATER TANK

Install gutters to channel rain from the roof into a tank or barrels to use to water the garden. Brew "compost tea" by diluting 1 part compost to 10 parts water or learn to make "tea bags" by filling paper or cloth bags with dried manure or compost, steeping in a watering can, and giving plants a boost every time you water.

STACK YOUR PLANTS

Layering is key in permaculture design. Use the taller trees as a canopy, shrubs for midlevels, and edibles for ground level.

PLAN BIG, START SMALL

Divide the landscape into zones to identify microclimates. Then gradually observe temperatures and growing habits in each zone over time.

Most of our modern plants are bred to appease our palates, keeping the sweet or mild and ignoring the healthy benefits of bitter and strong tasting. Tracing plants back to their heirloom ancestors reveals that vegetables have changed dramatically over thousands of years, which is why we are not always getting maximum benefit from the food we eat. Whether you are growing or buying vegetables, here are the top ten vegetables to select for optimally healthy eating.

1. GARLIC. Choose the deep-red–skinned varieties over all-white cloves and follow the ten-minute rule: smash the garlic and let it sit 10 minutes before you add it to a sauté pan. Sitting causes the key ingredient, allicin, to activate. Otherwise, the heat of cooking kills the allicin, and your garlic is merely a flavoring.

2. ONIONS. Choose red or yellow onions with pungent flavors that bring tears to your eyes. Onions that contain more sulfur are stronger in flavor than the sweeter types such as Vidalia or Walla Walla. In a 2004 study, extracts of strong onions destroyed 95 percent of human cancer cells in the liver and colon, while those of sweet onions killed only 10 percent.

3. BEETS. Heirloom Chioggia (candy-striped), golden, or white beets are beautiful to grow, sweeter in flavor, and contain qualities such as not "bleeding" in a salad. Yet a classic deep red beet that has been grown for centuries contains far more iron and betalains, plus has remarkable storage qualities for winter reserves.

4. CARROTS. It's a bit of a mystery how orange carrots captured the market, when purple carrots offer forty times more vitamin E than any other color. Purple carrots most closely resemble their wild ancestors, with red carrots coming in second place.

5. CRUCIFERS. Broccoli, cabbage, and kale are the most nutritious crops of all and are an excellent source of sulforaphenes, an anticancer compound. Most are slightly bitter, so wait until the temperatures drop below freezing for these veggies to turn flavorful.

6. LETTUCE. When choosing to grow lettuce, opt for red, reddish brown, purple, or dark green. Take it a step further to look for loose-leaf varieties and open butterheads over tight crisphead or iceberg lettuces.

7. PEAS. Eat the whole pod with snap or snow peas over traditional shelling peas if you seek maximum nutrients and fiber. Better yet, grow a range of different types of peas, one of the harbingers of spring and fall gardens.

8. POTATOES. Found in the Andes, the Peruvian purple potato was said to be the first, and over the centuries has been bred to be bigger, disease resistant, and eventually all white. Go back to the original for more flavor and more nutrients.

9. SALAD GREENS. Arugula, radicchio, endive, and spinach grow quickly year-round, and are ready for the salad bowl only a few weeks after the seeds are sown. Choose from the many varieties; all are easy to grow and offer trace nutrients that no scientist has bothered to measure, but you know they taste better than store-bought.

10. TOMATOES. Small is beautiful when it comes to healthy tomatoes, especially the tiny purple tomatoes that were found high in the Andes. Eventually bred to be larger and sweeter, the original tomato is somewhat sour but has four hundred times more lycopene than the average garden variety.

5

THE FRENCH HEIRLOOM GARDEN

EUROPEAN POTAGER STYLE

DESIGN NOTES

In this French kitchen garden, called a *potager*, you will find the best vegetables for cooks who love to garden: leeks, shallots, celeriac, carrots, and culinary herbs. Selecting specific heirloom varieties can make a difference between ordinary and extraordinary, and many French varieties are known to be superior in flavor.

INSPIRATION

The best-known example of a French kitchen garden on a large scale can be found in the Loire Valley at the Château de Villandry, where green cabbages, blue leeks, and jade carrot tops are artistically planted within geometric garden beds. Edged in boxwood, the garden is a pure celebration of history, aesthetics, and the necessity to grow food. The result is a tapestry of colors and textures to stimulate and enrich the visual appetite.

A rich heritage of French kitchen gardens can be traced back to Saint Fiacre, the patron saint of gardeners, whose reputation to engage with all creatures great and small is based on his initiative to plant a kitchen garden at a monastery to feed hungry patrons. Helped by a troupe of medieval monks, Saint Fiacre planted herbs, flowers, vegetables, and fruits intended for healing and nourishment. This first kitchen garden and those that followed served as a holy place for meditation and prayer, and as a retreat for the whole community.

Drawing from the past and bringing it into the future is the nature of this garden, featuring the best culinary European heirloom varieties, all open pollinated for the seed saver to continue the tradition year after year.

THE FRENCH HEIRLOOM GARDEN

DESIGN WISDOM
TIPS FOR GROWING

THINK LIKE AN ARTIST
Plant in blocks of color, using seeds and plants as your paintbrush. The vegetable garden is full of annuals, which are replanted each year, so be a food artist and use the garden as a blank canvas for your artistic ideas.

SET UP BOUNDARIES
Good fences make good gardens, keeping out predators and framing the garden like a beautiful picture. Consider planting a thick hornbeam or boxwood hedge to enclose the space and establish the perimeter of the garden.

OUTSIDE IN
Build a garden shed to serve as a potting shed, cold frame, and greenhouse for year-round growing, or as a quiet reading nook or hideaway.

STRONG BONES
Paths are the bones of the garden and give the whole design structure and balance. If done correctly, paths will keep weeds at bay and reduce the time and effort required to keep the garden neat and tidy. Hire a stonemason to install stone, brick, or cobblestone paths that will last many years into the future.

DRAW INSPIRATION
Often ideas come from other gardeners. Take time out for garden tours, visit historic sites with gardens, and fill your mind and your camera with photos for references to enhance your own design.

BE ROMANTIC
Plant fragrant roses, evening-scented stock, and Oriental lilies under the bedroom window or near the arbor. Carve out a comfortable sweet spot in the garden nook for sitting during the evening hours with moonflowers and nicotiana.

WELCOME VOLUNTEERS
Let flower pods go to seed in order to volunteer in paths and along the edges of the garden. While they may not be what you planned, they will soften the tight lines and formality, giving the garden more grace.

FLORA AND FAUNA
Medieval French gardens included hutches for rabbits, geese, ducks, guinea fowl, peacocks, and pheasants, so why not add a few soft, furry, or feathered friends of your own?

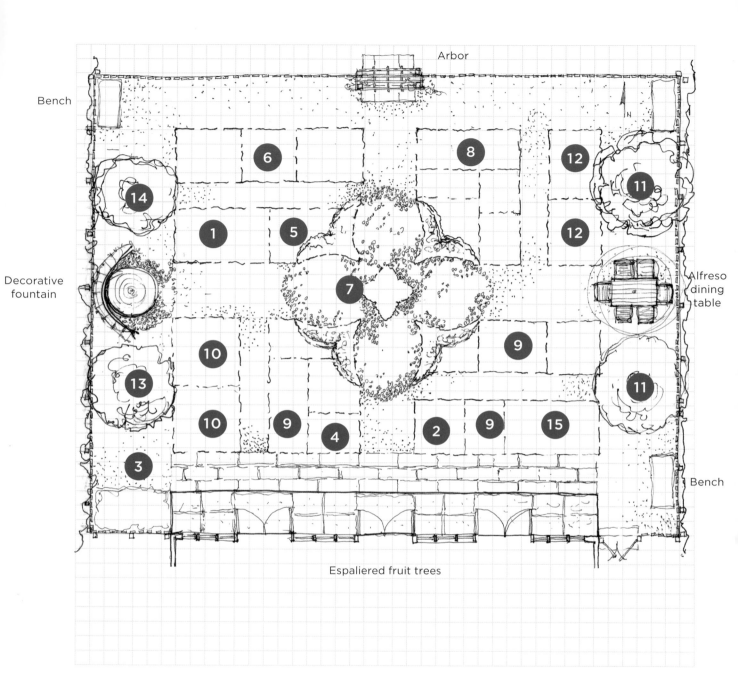

Bench

Arbor

Decorative fountain

Alfreso dining table

Bench

Espaliered fruit trees

PLANT KEY

☐ = 1 square foot

1. **BEAN:** Fin de Bagnols filet bean
2. **CARROT:** Touchon or Chantenay Red Core
3. **FLOWER:** Lilies of the valley
4. **FLOWER:** Nasturtium 'Moonlight'
5. **GREENS:** Mâche
6. **HERB:** French tarragon
7. **LAVENDER:** *Lavandula × intermedia* 'Provence'
8. **LEEK:** Blue Solaise

9. **LETTUCE:** Four Seasons
10. **MELON:** Charentais
11. **PLUM:** Mirabelle
12. **PUMPKIN:** Rouge Vif d'Etampes
13. **SHRUB:** French Lilac (*Syringa vulgaris*)
14. **SHRUB:** Mock orange (*Philadelphus × virginalis*)
15. **TOMATO:** Coeur de Boeuf (Oxheart)

SEED TALK

EDIBLE HEIRLOOM ARTIST ROSALIND CREASY

An acclaimed photographer and author of numerous edible gardening books, Rosalind Creasy began her career as a landscape designer. In 1984, she tore up her front yard in Palo Alto, California, to plant tomatoes, corn, and green beans, along with nasturtiums and zinnias. It shocked her neighbors, yet it also began the conversation about growing food, not lawns. When asked to design an edible garden for a restaurant, she put the garden not behind a tall fence but in a circle all around the restaurant on full view where guests could see the plants. She has been called the pioneer of the edible landscape movement and continues to advocate for growing heirlooms.

How did you get started as an edible gardener?

We moved to the West Coast in the seventies, and I immediately became involved in the environmental movement. I was aware that we were losing our prime agricultural soil to lawns and houses at an alarming rate. Gardening was all about chemicals and big business, and I got frustrated, which led me to take classes in landscape design so I could find a way to make changes from within the agricultural system.

How did change happen?

I was growing edibles and really excited to discover heirlooms because they offered varieties that were far more interesting than the seeds I was getting from the mainstream catalogs. I began to give lectures and show off my favorite heirlooms, yet received a lot of flak from seed companies for promoting heirlooms at my talks and in my books. They said I was putting seed companies and breeders out of business by teaching gardeners how to save seeds. It didn't stop me, and I still feel that heirlooms are far more interesting than hybrids, and gardeners are still buying plenty of seeds.

If you had to choose between flavor and nutrition, which would it be?

Flavor! If I don't like the taste, I am not going to eat it. I grew an heirloom white carrot and discovered it had a soapy taste. No wonder it is not popular! Early on, I learned how to taste vegetables and make comparisons between varieties at tasting events and in seed catalog trials and noticed that a carrot is not just a carrot. There is a wide flavor difference between varieties.

Why do you grow food and flowers together?

At first, I thought adding flowers to vegetable garden design might make growing food more appealing, but now I grow flowers for my bees and other beneficial insects. You have to have both, really. I've also learned from an entomologist that if I find aphids, I should leave them alone because they are food for the good bugs or predators to eat. For a healthy ecosystem, you have to allow the whole life cycle to work in the garden, which takes patience and observation.

What are some of your favorite heirlooms?

I've been a proud member of the Seed Savers Exchange since 1980 and have served on their board for two terms. Membership entitles you to have access to their vast network of seed savers who offer rare varieties not available from any other source. In my garden, you will always find Cherokee Purple tomato, Christmas lima bean, Boldog Hungarian spice pepper, Bull's Blood beet, rainbow chard, and plenty of Pacific Beauty calendula.

6

THE HERBS, GREENS, AND AROMATICS GARDEN

WILD AND CULTIVATED SALADS

DESIGN NOTES

Go beyond the ubiquitous mixed greens found in supermarkets to discover frilly lettuce, savory fennel, delicate chervil, and gorgeous rosettes of claytonia. Grow this garden for exceptional flavor and visually stunning, hard-to-find heirloom salad greens.

INSPIRATION

Consider this design as a starter garden for salad lovers, because as you explore the wide world of heirloom salad greens, a whole new world of food will open up. Begin with Italian arugula and radicchio, then move on to Asian tatsoi and shungiku, and garnish with French chervil and broadleaf cress for a tangy new twist.

Spicy, savory, bitter, and crisp are the qualities of mixed green leaves known as *mesclun*, a term derived from the French word *mesclar*, or "to mix." Mesclun can be composed of mostly bitter greens, including chicories, dandelions, arugula, spicy mustard, herbs, or sweeter leaves such as mâche, lettuce, and delicate flowers.

While most of us consider a green salad to be composed of lettuce, a mixture of wild greens such as leaves of claytonia, Goldgelber purslane, and Osaka purple mustard bring zingy flavor to the table. Mesclun packets offer mixed greens, yet in this garden, creating separate rows for each variety will allow the gardener to get to know favorites. Taste each green in the garden before tossing it with a dressing in a salad bowl.

THE HERBS, GREENS, AND AROMATICS GARDEN

DESIGN WISDOM
TIPS FOR GROWING

KEEP A SUCCESSION
For a continuation of greens from early spring to late fall, sow several rows every week. Follow a routine set down by Thomas Jefferson, who "planted a thimbleful [approximately one teaspoon] of greens every Monday morning."

TRY SOMETHING NEW
Go beyond your typical seed catalogs to discover the wide world of greens and try something different. If you are traveling to Europe or Asia, look for seed packets in the garden centers and nurseries to bring home to your own garden.

SOME LIKE IT HOT
Many greens that are grown past their prime taste hot and spicy in the garden yet can be tamed with a sweet creamy dressing. If you prefer milder-tasting greens, harvest them when they are small and tender.

WINDOW DRESSING
A window box full of herbs, greens, and aromatics is a welcome change from marigolds and zinnias, but make sure that your potting soil is organic if you plan to eat from it. What you feed your plants ultimately feeds you.

SOW EARLY
Greens love cool weather and germinate best when temperatures are below 80°F. Take advantage of the early spring and late fall to plant a crop of greens that will flourish during times other vegetables won't.

AVOID MIXED PACKETS
Mesclun is often sold as a packet of mixed seed, yet since each variety grows at a different rate, you won't get a balanced harvest. Alternatively, sow each variety in a separate row, mixing them together in the salad bowl instead. This will help you get to know what you like in the mix.

CUT AND COME AGAIN
Quite simply, "cut and come again" means harvesting the greens down to the soil line, leaving roots intact, watering, and waiting for another crop to sprout. Although not all greens are cut and come again, arugula will famously return but spicier with each successive harvest. Re-sow with fresh seeds after the second harvest for optimal flavor.

MIX AND MATCH
Make the most of the growing space in the garden, both high and low, by packing in as much planting material as possible. Greens and herbs adjust to tight areas, but plan to allow optimum conditions.

SEED TO SEED
Almost all plants ultimately go to flower, which produces seeds. Plan to save seeds for next year's garden, or allow them to drop on the ground to self-sow.

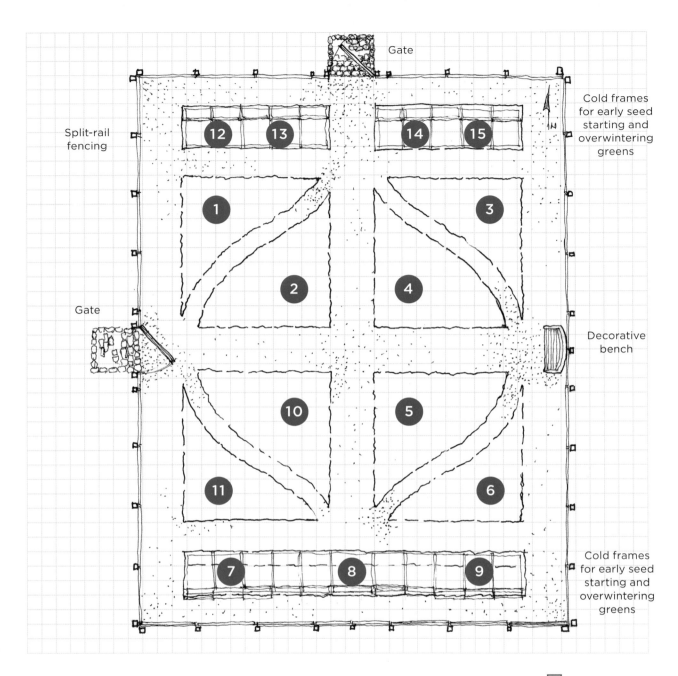

Gate

Cold frames
for early seed
starting and
overwintering
greens

Split-rail
fencing

Gate

Decorative
bench

Cold frames
for early seed
starting and
overwintering
greens

PLANT KEY

☐ = 1 square foot

1. **ARUGULA:** *Rucola selvatica*
2. **BASIL:** Opal
3. **BEET GREENS:** Bull's Blood
4. **CHERVIL:** Brussels Winter
5. **CLAYTONIA:** *Claytonia perfoliata*
6. **CRESS:** Wrinkled Crinkled
7. **FLOWER:** Borage
8. **FLOWER:** Calendula, Indian Prince

9. **FLOWER:** Nasturtium, Peach Melba
10. **LETTUCE:** Freckles
11. **LETTUCE:** Red Oak Leaf
12. **MÂCHE:** Vit
13. **MUSTARD:** Red Giant
14. **PURSLANE:** Goldgelber
15. **RADICCHIO:** Red Treviso

SEED TALK

HEIRLOOM SEED BREEDER FRANK MORTON

Around 1980, Frank Morton began growing a wild mix of salad greens on his organic farm in Philomath, Oregon, to sell to the local restaurants. After buying seeds from catalogs for several years, he branched off to start growing his own seeds; instead of harvesting plants to eat, he allowed the plants to mature and form seedpods. The result was a seed catalog called Wild Garden Seed, featuring hundreds of lettuces, salad greens, and aromatic herbs and edible flowers.

Wild Garden Seed continues to lead the way with innovative and unique seed varieties, though in 2002 Morton began something new: he wanted to share his knowledge of plant breeding and seed saving, so he began teaching others.

How did you come to start the catalog?

Originally, it was a self-sufficient impulse, something to keep us going because we were growing varieties that only we could produce. I had been quietly breeding and collecting seeds for decades. Finally, the time came when it was clearly time to stop growing salad greens and start producing seeds to sell, and the catalog business emerged in the early 1980s.

Why did you start teaching others to save seeds?

Preserving the diversity of plants was one consideration, but another was to encourage others to become seed savers and growers. The result is the emergence of farm-based seed growers who are producing specialty-seed catalogs much like my own. My work is to help other gardeners to become more self-sufficient and to develop a niche seed business of their own.

Why did you feel it was important to teach others?

I'm not sure, because I am essentially selling tickets to my competition, but I wanted to create an alternative to commercial seed growers, who are essentially contractors for seed-breeding companies, and they keep secrets. In the organic community, we all share information, so teaching and becoming a mentor made perfect sense.

Why did you start to offer flowers?

At farm conferences and workshops, we noticed a trend, especially among women farmers in their early twenties and thirties who were growing flowers for cutting. I had grown calendulas and poppies but wanted to figure out how to breed other flowers, so I began to grow everything, and quite honestly, went a little bit wild. Cleaning flower seeds can be much harder than those of vegetables, because they are all different shapes and sizes.

What are your favorite greens?

An underrated and little-known salad green is Upland cress, which grows year-round and is similar to watercress and more toothsome and spicier than arugula. Joker lettuce is a crisp green leaf splashed with red. Avalon Blue kale was bred on our farm. I also like White Russian kale and Red Herzog kale for salads. Chicory is finally becoming trendy, and Castelfranco and red Treviso radicchio are coming into the chef's repertoire. Brussels Winter chervil is my favorite for the salad bowl; I love the mild anise flavor and soft texture. My new favorite salad green is quinoa, harvested when the leaves are small, similar to lamb's-quarter, and it can tolerate hot weather. Let it grow and snap off the shoot when it is a foot tall, then harvest the stem and leaf together to break off like asparagus.

7

THE ITALIAN HEIRLOOM GARDEN

REGIONAL SPECIALTIES

DESIGN NOTES

Tasting Italian vegetables at the source is a wildly different experience from shopping for radicchio or artichokes at the grocery store. In this garden, you will grow regional favorites that reflect the true flavors and traditions of Italy as an homage to authentic cuisine while honoring Italian heirlooms.

INSPIRATION

It is no secret that the best way to experience true Italian cuisine is to visit Italy, which is why I signed up to take a weeklong cooking class with cookbook author Marcella Hazan in Venice. On the way to class, I chose the longest route through the Rialto Market, standing canalside and watching the farmers unload fava beans, fennel bulbs, red-skinned garlic, deep mahogany chicories, and purple artichokes from their gondolas. It was October, and the twisted leaves of the chicory Punterelle, piled next to dark purple eggplants and tawny onions, were a cook's paradise.

What I learned from the cooking class, and from Hazan's many cookbooks, is that what you keep out of a recipe is just as important as what you put in it. On the first day of class, we learned that the proper Italian way to cook simply starts by stocking your pantry with quality olive oil, Parmigiano-Reggiano, prosciutto, anchovies, and all of the other key elements that make Italian cuisine so inviting. A basket of freshly harvested vegetables, whether from the market or from your garden, will sing with flavor if you start with good ingredients.

This Italian heirloom garden design includes a brick oven to slow down the pace of life. Pour the red wine and turn your Italian garden into a gathering place for entertaining and lingering with friends.

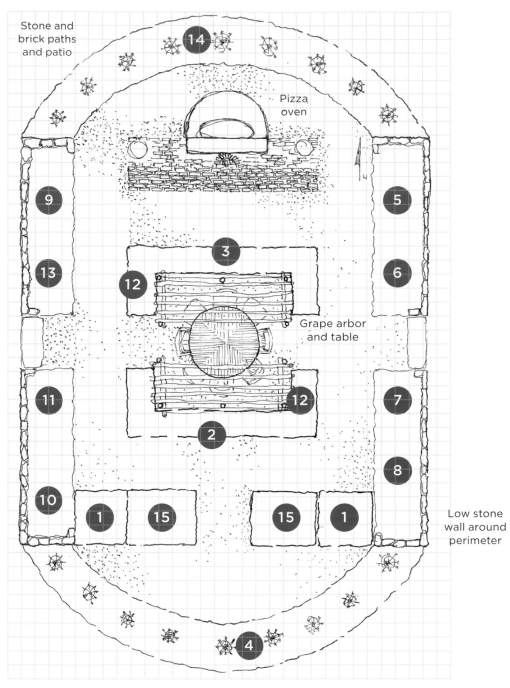

Stone and brick paths and patio

Pizza oven

Grape arbor and table

Low stone wall around perimeter

PLANT KEY

☐ = 1 square foot

1. **ARTICHOKE:** Violetta di Chioggia
2. **ARUGULA:** Selvatica
3. **BASIL:** Italiano Classico (Sweet Genovese)
4. **BEAN:** Borlotto or cranberry
5. **BEET:** Chioggia

6. **BROCCOLI RAAB:** Cima di Rapa
7. **EGGPLANT:** Violetta Lunga
8. **ENDIVE:** Broad-Leaved Batavian
9. **FENNEL:** Florence
10. **KALE:** Blue Lacinato
11. **ONION:** Red Torpedo

12. **PEPPER:** Corno di Toro
13. **RADICCHIO:** Rossa di Treviso or Early Treviso
14. **TOMATO:** San Marzano
15. **ZUCCHINI:** Costata Romanesco

THE ITALIAN HEIRLOOM GARDEN

DESIGN WISDOM
TIPS FOR GROWING

SEEK THE AUTHENTIC

While the terroir may not be Italy, the Italian vegetables you grow will reflect a genuine quality if you start with authentic seeds.

GEO BEE

Most Italian heirloom vegetables are named after the regions where they origi- nated. Get out a map and get to know Italian geography by following what you are growing. Then match the vegetable to a recipe from the local cuisine.

LIVE OUTDOORS

Entertain in the garden with an outdoor brick oven. Build it yourself or hire a mason; either way, you'll find yourself spending more time in the garden—at play and not at work.

MAKE CORNERS COUNT

Construct a trellis or arbor in the corners of the garden for growing flowering vines, runner beans, or grapes, or to create a shady nook to hide in during the heat of the day.

HIGH-LOW

Stagger plants of varying heights to make the most of a garden bed. Find partners that can grow in the same space, one down low while the other reaches tall.

BAMBOOZLE

There is nothing more beautiful than natural bamboo used for trellising pole beans, staking tomatoes, or weaving a screen or fence. Grow it yourself, or buy poles in 4- to 8-foot lengths.

LEARN TECHNIQUES

Italian gardeners enjoy the challenge of cultivating hard-to-grow vegetables, and if you grew up in an Italian family, these techniques may have been passed down to you; if not, be prepared to do some research and learn something new.

CRAZY FOR CHICORY

Acquire a taste for the bitter leaf of chicory. Adding bitter to your diet helps clear toxins and aids digestion. Chicory, in all its shapes and forms, is an underappreci- ated green and adds vibrant flavor and beauty to salads.

SEED TALK

HEIRLOOM SEED HISTORIAN DR. WILLIAM WOYS WEAVER

Dr. William Woys Weaver wrote the book *Heirloom Vegetable Gardening* in 1997 (updated in 2018) and became an instant celebrity in the food-and-garden world. The book opened a conversation about growing your own food for flavor and saving the seeds that carry historical value. As both a food historian and a storyteller, Weaver brought a new awareness of one factor about heirloom seeds that had been largely overlooked: memories. His interest in heirlooms and the seed collection he calls Roughwood was sparked when he opened his grandparents' freezer to find bags of frozen seeds that had been in storage for decades.

How did your grandfather begin his seed collection?

My grandfather, H. Ralph Weaver [1896–1956], grew food on two acres in West Chester, Pennsylvania. Food was scarce during the Depression, but he set out to feed the family, as well as anyone who showed up at their table. One frequent visitor was painter Horace Pippin, an African American who brought seeds to trade for apitherapy treatments administered [through honeybee stings] by my grandfather. This was the start of his seed collection, and he sought other seeds from his Pennsylvania Dutch neighbors and fellow Quakers.

It wasn't until after his death that I discovered the seeds. I was in college, ten years after he died, and I found them in the depths of their chest freezer, sealed in jars. My grandfather was light-years ahead of me concerning what you do with seeds to preserve them, and I learned this the hard way, because opening the jars instantly began to destroy the seeds' viability.

What do you know about your grandfather?

He was like me—he collected orchids, kept pigeons, was always involved in everything. It had nothing to do with biodiversity or the environmental reasons that we choose to save seeds now, but he had a nose for rare things. And he recognized that Horace Pippin's seeds were special. The more I learned about my grandparents through these seeds, the more interested I became in the story of their lives. At the pit of the Depression, they built their house and had a lot of relatives out of work, with no money. My grandfather had two acres behind the house, got seeds from relatives, and started to grow food to feed them all.

How did Roughwood Seed Collection get started?

In 1979, I moved into a house formerly owned by Thomas Biddle, who named the house Roughwood after an ancestral home in Scotland. I grew a large *jardin potager* [kitchen garden] and sowed many of my grandfather's seeds and others that I had collected to write about in *Heirloom Vegetable Gardening*.

What do you love most about being a seed saver?

Seeds are food waiting to happen, because you can't eat without seeds. Everybody else looks at seeds as an agricultural asset. I say no, they are not mummies in a museum. Seeds are about life and cultural patrimony that belongs to all of us. Seeds contain memories of the food and the history of people and civilizations.

You have written books on ephemera. Explain how this relates to seed saving.

Here today, gone tomorrow. Unless we preserve something, it will disappear. When you save a seed, it will be a part of the living history of the present once it is grown in the garden.

AUTUMN APPLES.

state. Fruit above the medium size, roundish, scarcely flattened, fair, and well formed. Skin, when fully ripe, pale yellow or straw colour. Stalk about an inch long, slender at its junction with the fruit. Calyx closed, and set in a basin of moderate depth. Flesh tender, sweet, rich and excellent. The tree is a pretty free grower, and bears large crops. This we think will prove a valuable sort. Ripe in August and September.

41. GRAVENSTEIN. § Thomp. Lind.
Grave Stije.

A superb looking German apple, which originated at Gravenstein, in Holstein, and is thought one of the finest apples of the north of Europe. It fully sustains its reputation here, and is, unquestionably, a fruit of first rate quality. Fruit large, rather flattened, and a little one sided or angular, broadest at the base.

Fig. 32. *Gravenstein.*

Stalk quite short and strong, deeply set
deep, rather irregular basin. Skin s...
becoming bright yellow, and beau...
and marbled with light and deep...
and crisp, with a high flavo...
Ripens with us in Septembe...
longer. The trees are v...
young.

APPLES.

size, oval, very regular in shape, rather b...
Eye sunk in an even hollow. Stalk sho...
planted. Skin deep yellow, freckled with nu...
Flesh pale yellow, crisp, tender, with a fine...
vour. The tree grows freely, and forms an u...

38. FALL HARVEY. § Man. Ken...

A fine large Fall fruit from Essex co., Mass., very...
teemed in that neighbourhood. We do not think it c...
to the Fall pippin, which it a little resembles. Fle...
Fruit large, a little flattened, obscurely ribbed or ir...
about the stalk, which is rather slender, an inch long, set...
wide, deep cavity. Calyx closed, small, in a rather shal...
basin. Skin pale straw yellow, with a few scattered dots. Fle...
white, juicy, crisp, with a rich, good flavour. October and No...vember.

39. FALL PIPPIN. § Coxe. Floy.

ll Pippin is, we think, decidedly an American variety,
and Lindley to the contrary, notwithstanding. It is,
a seedling raised in this country, from the White
or the Holland pippin, both of which it so
from which it in fact, differs most strongly
The Fall Pippin is a noble fruit, and
Autumn apples in the middle states,
and its delicious flavour for the table
ally a little flattened, pretty
the eye. Stalk rather
considerably beyond
Holland Pippin,) set in a
not very large,
Skin smooth,
a tinge of
red dots
the fla

8

THE NEW AMERICAN HEIRLOOM GARDEN

PRESERVING HISTORY

DESIGN NOTES

Finding eighteenth-century seeds for heirloom treasures requires a bit of a search these days yet provides a chance to rediscover some of Thomas Jefferson's favorites. This plan reflects the familiar formality found at Monticello, with the fluidity of a modern heirloom design.

INSPIRATION

On March 17, 1809, retired president Thomas Jefferson departed Washington with seeds purchased from a local seed man named Theophilus Holt. Six days later, he started planting peas, and thus began his "Kalendar," or garden book, that would document the seasonal progress of each vegetable.

Jefferson drew inspiration for his flower and vegetable gardens at Monticello from the ones he visited in France and England. Over time, he grew more than 330 varieties of vegetables and herbs from 99 species, readily admitting in his journals that there were more failures than successes. For Jefferson, seeds became a form of currency to share with fellow gardeners all over the world. He preserved his seeds in a unique rack he designed that held hundreds of glass vials sealed with corks, and that would be rolled into a closet near his study during the off-season and out into the garden at planting time.

Inspired by a traditional Virginia block-style garden with long, straight rows and the timeless design of the Monticello kitchen garden, the use of curved walls and a pavilion balanced by formal geometric shapes in each of the beds gives the overall design structure.

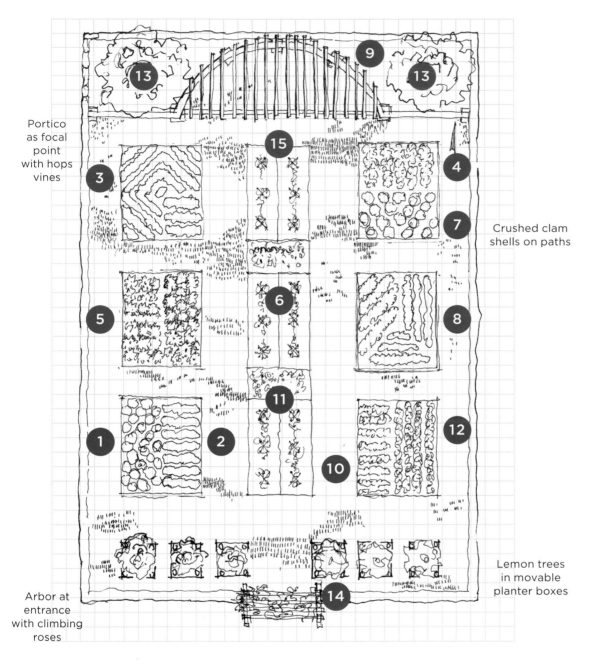

Portico as focal point with hops vines

Crushed clam shells on paths

Lemon trees in movable planter boxes

Arbor at entrance with climbing roses

PLANT KEY

☐ = 1 square foot

1. **FLOWER:** *Amaranthus tricolor* Joseph's Coat
2. **FLOWER:** *Monarda didyma* Jacob Cline
3. **BEAN:** Bush-type Broad Windsor fava
4. **COLLARDS:** Vates or Champion
5. **CUCUMBER:** Lemon
6. **POLE BEAN:** Sieva Carolina lima
7. **KALE:** Siberian
8. **LETTUCE:** Tennis Ball and Brown Dutch

9. **HOPS VINE:** Cascade or Chinosa
10. **OKRA:** Cajun Jewel
11. **PEA:** Green Arrow
12. **PEPPER:** McMahon's Texas Bird
13. **SEA KALE:** Crambe Maritima
14. **SWEET PEA:** Painted Lady
15. **TOMATO:** Purple Calabash

THE NEW AMERICAN HEIRLOOM GARDEN

LOVE MULCH

Mulch provides protection to plant roots from summer heat, cuts back on water use, and prevents weeds. Look for a natural material: straw, salt hay, or chopped leaves.

CONSERVE WATER

Consider installing drip irrigation before planting this garden to provide water directly to the plants' roots. Plan to cover the plastic tubing with mulch.

SAVE SEEDS

Allow the most robust plants to mature to seedpod stage, then collect the seeds. Dry and pack them into glass jars or paper envelopes, labeled with the date and varietal details.

NATURAL PATHS

Mulch the paths to keep the weeds down. What you use for path material depends on the style of your garden. Allow enough width between the beds to fit a wheelbarrow and to walk two by two.

ELEGANT TUTEURS

In keeping with the elegance of Monticello, add a formal structure for growing vining plants, often called a *tuteur*, which can be left natural or painted. It can be decorative or useful—to hold up tomatoes, pole beans, or any type of ornamental vine.

PLANTER BOXES

At Monticello, planter boxes with lemon and lime trees were grown outdoors and then brought indoors for the winter. Consider adding a row of planter boxes to grow fruiting trees that can be wheeled into the house for winter.

CREATE ORDER

An essential step to keeping the gardener and the garden efficient is to keep the garden neat and tidy. A garden planted in geometric grids is pleasing to the eye and easier to maintain.

GARDEN JOURNAL

Thomas Jefferson was known for his meticulously detailed garden journals. Looking back on notes about the weather, germination success, and other observations may be helpful and improve your gardening techniques.

SEED TALK

MONTICELLO HISTORIC GARDENER PETER HATCH

Peter Hatch is the author of *A Rich Spot on Earth: Thomas Jefferson's Revolutionary Garden at Monticello,* an extraordinary history full of rich details on the origins of Monticello's 1,000-foot-long terraced garden, and the plants and the philosophy behind the third President's garden passion. For thirty-five years, Hatch was the Director of Gardens and Grounds at Monticello, responsible for, among other duties, restoring Jefferson's eight-acre fruit and vegetable garden. With the help of Jefferson's remarkable garden notes as well as years of archaeological excavations, the original layout took shape in 1984, and is considered one of the most accurate garden restorations of its kind. Monticello, which now attracts hundreds of thousands of visitors each year, maintains one of the most inspiring and iconic kitchen gardens in American history.

What do you think Jefferson would say about GMO seeds?

Thomas Jefferson was an ambiguous figure; he is all things to all people, and when we say "today Jefferson would do this or do that," we are often just talking about ourselves. He loved science and technology, so he would have been a great advocate for many of the things happening today in both areas, such as internet technology and possibly GMOs (genetically modified organisms) because both involve new advances in science. On the other hand, he was a naturalist who loved to eat his vegetables, believed in the natural order of things, and even carried the banner of the organic gardening movement. So it is hard to say how he would respond to advanced plant breeding and GMO seeds. Would he embrace machine technology or would he become a "back to the lander"? It is an interesting debate.

What did Monticello look like when you were hired in 1977?

Compared to where I had been working previously, a historic site with very high professional preservation and education standards, Monticello was a flashback to an earlier era. The standard tour for the general public showed only the inside of Jefferson's house, with all of what were considered his inventions, and a flower garden that had been accurately restored by the Garden Club of Virginia but without a regard for historic flower species. Now, the kitchen gardens are integrated into the full story of the place and are an important attraction for visitors.

How did you know how to reconstruct the kitchen gardens?

Before we could start any work on the terraced garden and orchard, Monticello hired an archeological crew to confirm Jefferson's extensive notes about the character of the garden and to preserve any historical artifacts or information that might be lingering under the surface. Over some three years, archaeologists identified the precise location of fifty-nine of the original Jefferson-era fruit trees, uncovered a 1,000-foot-long retaining wall, traced the path of a 4,000-foot-long, 10-foot-high fence, and found the remains of the foundation for Jefferson's garden pavilion. These were significant discoveries and helped us to re-create the garden with meticulous detail.

Why did Jefferson note so many failures in his "Garden Kalendar"?

Jefferson retired from the Presidency in 1809 and returned to Monticello to find the completion of the garden terrace, carved from the hillside by a crew of seven enslaved African-Americans. His first growing season was a tough year because there was no rain. I often say few gardeners failed as often as Thomas Jefferson; he once wrote if he failed 99 times out of a 100, the one success was worth the 99 failures. He was an experimenter, unrelenting in his effort to overcome one catastrophe after another, a reflection of his experiential, scientific, and Enlightenment aesthetic. He wrote that in gardening, "the failure of one thing is replaced by the success of another."

Where did Thomas Jefferson find sources for seeds and plants?

Jefferson wrote, "the greatest service which can be rendered any country is to add a useful plant to its culture." He documented the planting of some 330 varieties of vegetables and 170 types of fruit, and Monticello was an "Ellis Island" of plants introduced from around the world. Jefferson was a "seedy missionary" of useful garden plants, and he exchanged seeds with most of the leading horticulturists in Europe and the United States, as well as with friends and fellow political figures. A lifelong seed saver, he designed a seed rack, with glass vials and cork stoppers, that was stored in his study and carried out to the garden site at planting time. He also had propagation nurseries in which precious seeds were planted and fruit trees grafted.

What would have been some of Thomas Jefferson's favorites?

SEA KALE: Grown and eaten like broccoli. Clay pots were used to cover the emerging plants in late winter. This blanched the stems to keep them tender.

LIMA BEANS: Sieva pole is a classic Southern favorite; vigorous vines are staked on tepees in the center of the garden. Growing beans this way takes up less space than traditional bush beans.

SHELLING PEAS: These are considered to be his favorite vegetable, and Jefferson engaged in a neighborhood competition to see who could harvest the first spring pea. The winner would then host a dinner.

ASPARAGUS BEANS: Also known as long beans, these grow to be a foot long. It's a vigorous climbing vine, and the pods hang in groups of two or more.

EGGPLANTS: These plants were still foreign to most gardeners during Jefferson's era. His enslaved chef, Peter Hemings, was given seeds by a neighbor as well as directions on how to prepare the fruit. Jefferson grew "white," "purple," and "prickly" varieties of eggplant in adjacent rows.

OKRA: The Jefferson family manuscripts include a recipe for "okra soup," or gumbo. It included an international array of vegetables: okra from Africa, tomatoes and potatoes from South America, and lima beans and "cymlins" from Native American gardens.

TOMATOES: Jefferson was one of the first to introduce tomatoes to American gardeners. Recipes for tomato omelets, gazpacho, and catsup reside in the Jefferson family manuscripts.

9

THE NEW HEIRLOOM FLOWER GARDEN

PRESERVING BEAUTY

DESIGN NOTES

Wafting fragrance and meandering paths; the delicate sound of a water fountain; the welcoming sight of a bench to encourage you to sit and linger. Grow a collection of old-fashioned flowers in pastel shades of blue, pink, and purple, decorated by a low border of germander to make it easy to harvest a bouquet.

INSPIRATION

Instinct makes us lean in toward a flower to smell its fragrance, yet too often the bouquet is made with modern flowers, which are fragrance-free. Scent originates from the petals, designed to draw the pollinator inside of a blossom to fertilize the pollen that will result in a seed. Plant breeders have been improving heirloom flowers, leading to catalog descriptions that read "pollen-less" or "long lasting" or "long stemmed," which are all desirable if you are strictly a flower arranger. For the gardener, however, there is nothing like fragrance to liven up the flower garden.

This garden design is filled with old-fashioned favorites that go back centuries and will freshen your landscape with fragrance both day and night. Nicotiana and moonflower emit vanilla-scented perfume in the evening; sweet peas are reminiscent of clove, and the long stems make a wonderful cut flower; and agastache and sweet William are magnets for bees. Other flowers in this collection are grown for their unusual form especially prized in a flower arrangement.

THE NEW HEIRLOOM FLOWER GARDEN

DESIGN WISDOM
TIPS FOR GROWING

BE BEE FRIENDLY

Planting old-fashioned open-pollinated flowers encourages a wide range of beneficial bees and keeps the vegetable garden and fruit trees abundantly productive.

BECOME A BEEKEEPER

Set up a backyard hive to bring honeybees into your garden. Mason bees require less maintenance; set up a wild area with hollowed bamboo or cardboard tubes for them to build nests with mud and hay.

ENCOURAGE DIVERSITY

Plant flowers that bloom at different times, with a range of heights and plant types to provide a variety of pollen- and nectar-rich blooms throughout a longer season.

SUPPORT THE SAFE SEED PLEDGE

Many seed catalogs carry the Safe Seed Pledge to signal their opposition to genetically engineered seeds and plants. Support these companies that promote safe and genetically stable seeds for future generations.

SOW SEEDS INDOORS

For a jump-start on the summer season, sow seeds indoors to grow in a sunny window and set out after the frost-free date.

KEEP CUTTING

Annuals respond to frequent cutting and will grow into bushy, vigorous plants when they are continually harvested. Cut just above a flower node to encourage branching growth.

KEEP DEAD-HEADING

Remove faded blossoms to encourage new buds and flowers to appear. When flowers remain on the plant past their prime, they drain energy away from the plant and trigger it to stop producing flowers.

TRY SOMETHING NEW THAT IS OLD

Dig deep into the past with vintage seed catalogs to see what gardeners grew in a different era. These old-fashioned beauties may be hard to find but are worth the effort to establish a new source, rather than relying on the ordinary.

GO OUT AT NIGHT

Place a bench in the garden near night-blooming flowers. Not only will you enjoy the wafting fragrance, but you may even be lucky enough to observe nocturnal pollinators.

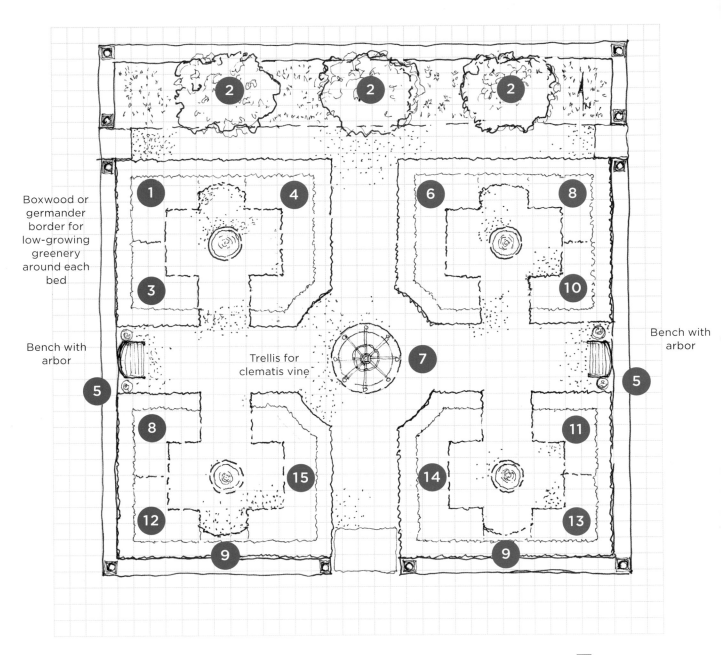

Boxwood or germander border for low-growing greenery around each bed

Bench with arbor

Bench with arbor

Trellis for clematis vine

PLANT KEY

☐ = 1 square foot

1. **VERBENA:** *Verbena bonariensis*
2. **RUGOSA ROSE:** Blanc Double de Coubert
3. **KISS-ME-OVER-THE-GARDEN-GATE:** *Polygonum orientale* Ladyfingers
4. **LARKSPUR:** *Delphinium grandiflorum* Blue Mirror
5. **MOONFLOWER VINE:** *Ipomea alba* Alba
6. **NICOTIANA:** *Nicotiana sylvestris*
7. **SWEET AUTUMN CLEMATIS:** *Clematis paniculata*
8. **POPPY:** *Papaver somniferum* Hungarian Blue Breadseed

9. **SWEET PEA:** *Lathyrus odoratus* Cupani
10. **SWEET WILLIAM:** *Dianthus barbatus*
11. **TASSEL FLOWER:** *Emilia javanica*
12. **TITHONIA:** *Tithonia rotundifolia* Mexican sunflower
13. **STOCK:** Evening-scented *Matthiola longipetala bicornis*
14. **SNAPDRAGON:** *Antirrhinum majus nanum* Black Knight
15. **DAHLIA:** Café au Lait (dinnerplate type)

SEED TALK

HEIRLOOM FLOWER CATALOG FOUNDER MARILYN BARLOW

"What is an antique flower?" asks Marilyn Barlow, the founder and owner of Select Seeds, in the introduction to her seed catalog listing more than five hundred varieties of antique and heirloom flowers. Her mission is to lure you into this colorful and fragrant world and convince you to grow a clutch of sweet and spicy nasturtiums, clove-scented sweet peas, or evening-scented stock.

Barlow was lucky to grow up in a garden that had once been her grandfather's, which meant that she already knew a thing or two about flowers long before she could reel off the Latin names. Through pure curiosity and doggedness to find the hard to find, her business is built on her personal favorites and is a valuable resource for heirloom flowers. Select Seeds is a farm-based business that her daughter, Allison, now helps keep running smoothly.

Did you grow up in a gardening family?

Our home had been in our family since 1855, a Victorian farmhouse that was built by a member of our family and passed down several generations. All were avid gardeners, and because my great-grandfather was a wonderful naturalist, he built pools and rock gardens for the flowers, yet most were gone by the time I came along. What survived, however, were the hardy perennials. Oriental poppies, iris, lilies, primroses, and hay-scented ferns were some of my favorites.

How did you happen to start your seed catalog business?

When we bought our property in Union, Connecticut, we purchased fifty acres with an old 1835 Cape house. To start our garden, we began to search for the perennials from my youth, but it was an era when the focus of most garden centers was on compact dwarf bedding plants. Most of the old-fashioned flowers that I sought were tall and lanky, with striking fragrance, and I could not find sources of seed anywhere. I did find sources for seed in Europe, however, where they still valued these old-fashioned beauties, and began to import seeds for my garden and to resell.

What were the criteria for the flowers in your first catalog?

I focused on any flower grown prior to the 1950s that was open-pollinated and preferably fragrant. In 1987, I mailed out a tiny leaflet that had a listing of flower seeds to customers who responded to a classified ad I placed in garden magazines. I did not have any idea that old-fashioned flowers would be popular, and the catalog is now full color and has grown into a far larger business than I ever anticipated.

What are some of your favorite heirloom flowers?

My garden would not be complete without heirloom peonies. Although the ones around my house have no name, they have a fragrance that makes me weak at the knees. I also grow heliotrope, especially the tall old-fashioned type, not the dwarf bedding plant. It was once hugely popular in the Victorian era, yet has largely fallen by the wayside. Another favorite is a variety called Tithonia, also known as 'Torch'. It has brilliant scarlet orange flowers atop fluted stems. Monarchs and other butterflies love it; it blooms late, when the butterflies are coming through. Basket flower is a native annual with huge white and lavender blooms that are honey scented. Sweet mignonette is an old-fashioned beauty that blooms from July to November without ever being cut back; it's sweetly scented, as is sweet alyssum, with honey-scented blossoms that honeybees adore.

ALYSSUM: SWEET WHITE

Circa 1828

Swoon over the honey-scented blossoms of sweet alyssum, a magnet for bees and other pollinators. It thrives in small spaces and containers. Sow seeds in between patio stones for a soft ornamental carpet for your bare feet to enjoy. Pairs well with nigella and larkspur.

BACHELOR'S BUTTON (*Centaurea cyanus*)

Circa 1806

Planning a wedding? Sow seeds for all-blue bachelor's button, a classic boutonniere for the groom and for the bride's bouquet. Strong stems that turn even more vigorous with each cut, all-blue bachelor's button continues to live up to its reputation as a flower grower's favorite, with excellent productivity and reliability. Pairs well with lavatera and calendula in the vase or the garden.

DAME'S ROCKET (*Hesperis*)

Circa 1807

Known as wild phlox, dame's rocket is best suited for the back border or wooded edges, but can become invasive. Once it's in bloom, the whiff of sweet honey will catch you off guard. After blooming, dame's rocket seed may escape into the meadows to delight the eye with an ocean of deep lilac flowers in early spring.

GLOBE GILIA

Circa 1826

Add a traditional twist to the flower border with globe gilia, tiny spheres of individual blue flowers. It contributes colorful accents in a garden with bright California poppies or calendula. Sow a large block for a profusion of nodding heads. Drought tolerant and can take some shade.

LARKSPUR—ROCKET (*Blue*)

Circa 1912

Nothing says "cottage garden" better than ruffled romantic larkspur, a diminutive form of delphinium that requires no staking. The crisp blue flowers are exquisite in a bride's bouquet. While cherished for its freshness, larkspur also dries beautifully for a wedding keepsake. Combine with pink lavatera and nigella.

HOLLYHOCK: SINGLE MIXED COLORS

Circa 1831

In the not-so-distant past, hollyhocks were known as the outhouse flower, a useful plant to cordon off areas for a bit of privacy. Hollyhocks remain a cottage garden classic, relatively easy to start from seed yet requiring patience. A biennial that takes two years to grow from seed, hollyhock blooms the second year.

10

THE SEED SAVER'S GARDEN

FULL CIRCLE

DESIGN NOTES

The first time you save seeds from your garden to share with friends or swap at a seed exchange, you might wonder why you have not tried this before. The results are worth the small effort it takes to collect the seedpods.

INSPIRATION

Seeds are fragile living organisms and one of nature's resources that is available to everyone for free. When you save seeds you can easily grow enough to also give away to other gardeners, like a good sourdough-bread starter. Seeds have crossed the ocean and traveled from garden to garden and hand to hand. At one time, everyone from Benjamin Franklin to Thomas Jefferson was a seed saver, eager to seek out new varieties from around the world.

When seed catalogs were introduced in the early 1800s, people began to enjoy the convenience of buying seeds through the mail. Early pioneers traveling across the country yearned for the annual catalog to arrive, which served as a growing guide and resource. By the early twentieth century, however, the seed industry shifted from catering to home gardeners to selling to market growers. Seed catalogs began to drop regional favorites to cater to farmers whose interest was higher yields.

Join the ranks of seed savers throughout the world who are collectively growing open-pollinated seeds for the future.

Brick or stone entrances with
morning glory arbors

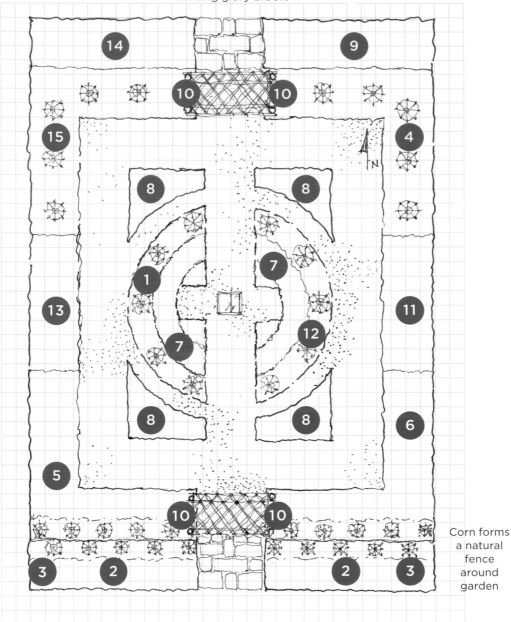

Corn forms
a natural
fence
around
garden

PLANT KEY

☐ = 1 square foot

1. **BEAN:** Christmas lima bean
2. **CALENDULA:** Flashback
3. **CORN:** Popping Corn Dakota Black
4. **CUCUMBER:** Boston Pickling
5. **FLOWER:** Zinnia (*Pumila*) Cut and Come Again
6. **FLOWER:** Cosmos Seashell
7. **FLOWER:** Bachelor's button Blue Boy
8. **LETTUCE:** Deer Tongue

9. **MELON:** Moon and Stars (watermelon)
10. **MORNING GLORY:** Grandpa Ott's
11. **ONION:** Egyptian walking
12. **PEA:** Lincoln shelling pea
13. **PEPPER:** Jimmy Nardello
14. **PUMPKIN:** Galeux d'Eysines
15. **TOMATO:** Brandywine

THE SEED SAVER'S GARDEN

DESIGN WISDOM
TIPS FOR GROWING

BUY LOCAL SEEDS

Choose to spend your seed dollars at smaller regional seed companies, which value and recognize the importance of saving seeds and preserving heirloom and open-pollinated varieties.

FIND A SEED LIBRARY

A true seed library lends or shares seed with gardeners, with the agreement that seeds will be grown and then returned as fresh seeds at the end of the season. This method keeps the supplies current and vigorous while allowing the community to grow food and flowers for free.

SEED SAVER BOX

Keep your seeds viable by storing them in an airtight seed box. Be sure to label each variety with name, date, where it was grown, and the origin of the seeds. Store in a dark, dry place with cool temperatures that do not fluctuate.

PROTECT FROM FROST

Seed-saving requires plants to grow to full maturity. If frosty temperatures threaten to strike before the seeds have matured, be prepared to cover the plant with fabric to protect the seed heads from freezing.

BUILD YOUR OWN LIBRARY

Saving seeds will differ among each plant type; some are easy while others are more complicated. There are plenty of great resources available to teach you the best way to save and store seeds.

BECOME EDUCATED

Learn about genetically modified organisms (GMOs) and how genetic diversity can threaten or enhance food crops. What are the effects on the health of plants, people, and the environment? Do you have concerns about pollinators? Speak up!

SEED EXCHANGES

Invite friends to gather and exchange saved seeds or purchase seeds in a bulk order. Provide paper envelopes and spill out the seeds into a glass jar to scoop and share, or prepackage small amounts.

SEED TALK

When Lee Buttala became a seed-saving expert, it was not to save the world but to rescue the Black Barlow columbine seed from extinction. "I was greedy," he says. "It was hard to find seed, and I wanted more plants." As the leader of Seed Savers Exchange, he has come to appreciate the many reasons why people save seeds.

Seed Savers Exchange started with just thirty-nine members and now has over thirteen thousand members worldwide. The headquarters for the exchange is at Heritage Farm, located six miles from Decorah, Iowa. It is the largest nongovernment seed bank in the United States, and its mission is to preserve the diverse garden heritage of seeds for future generations.

When we spoke by phone, he had just returned from a mission to take seeds to the Svalbard Global Seed Vault in Norway, founded by Dr. Cary Fowler, which contains seeds from every country around the world as insurance that there will be a future for seeds.

What was it like to be in the Svalbard Global Seed Vault in Norway?

Being in the vault and looking at seeds from North and South Korea, Africa, and Asia, all side by side, was evidence that we all come together in the garden, and our common vocabulary is seeds. Like a Thanksgiving table, seeds can bring us together in the moment, without politics. I almost cried, but it was seventeen degrees below zero and my tears would have frozen.

What did you take to Svalbard?

Seed Savers Exchange is the only non-government-supported source for open-pollinated and heirloom seeds that contributes to the seed vault. We grow out between six hundred and one thousand varieties each year, adding seed samples from our freshest crop. We grow a wide range of beans, corn, and squash, and along with these seeds, we preserve the stories, as they are part of the legacy of these varieties and of us as a people. We document the histories for many of the twenty-five thousand varieties maintained in our seed bank at Heritage Farm.

Why is seed saving important for all of us?

Seed saving is a twofold process. It is mission-driven because it is important to build up and maintain what we have, and also to distribute to home gardeners and make sure these seeds are being used and kept for the long term. It's not just about holding on to the past but creating a new future. People are allowing us to keep heirloom varieties where they belong: in our gardens and on our tables.

How is Seed Savers Exchange different from other seed catalogs?

A seed has the capacity to be mnemonic, to contain memories of people, places, food, and fragrance. While our mission is to preserve seeds and to capture the stories associated with the seed, we also aim to keep them in circulation for the future. We grow seed at Heritage Farm so you don't have to, because realistically it is a lot of work and requires specific isolation for controlled growing areas to avoid cross-pollination. We want to make sure that gardeners will keep these crops alive and thriving in their gardens.

While all heirloom seeds are open pollinated, heirlooms can also be traced back to a story. Often they are named after a person who saved the seed or a place where the seed was found growing. Here are three stories of heirloom seeds that were rescued and are now readily available through seed catalogs.

MORNING GLORY: *Grandpa Ott's*

In 1972, John Ott gave seeds for this purple morning glory to his granddaughter Diane Whealy, cofounder of the Seed Savers Exchange. He had brought them from his homeland of Bavaria, Germany, and when Whealy grew them out, she found the variety with its deep-purple flowers and distinctive small red star on the throat to be a prolific bloomer on vigorous vines. She saved the seeds each year until there were enough to share with others to package and sell through the Seed Savers catalog. Morning glories can easily become an invasive weed, and are best grown in areas where they can be controlled, not among vegetables, since they are not edible.

HUSK GROUND-CHERRY: *Aunt Molly's*

This Polish heirloom from 1837 tastes like pineapple and toasted caramel, with a nice hint of tartness. The size of cherry tomatoes, the tiny fruits are enclosed in brown papery husks, and drop to the ground when fully ripe. High in natural pectin, they are a good choice for preserves and are widely found in gardens among the Pennsylvania Dutch community. As with many heirlooms, the story of how this one got its name varies. One story claims seed saver Suzanne Ashworth, author of *Seed to Seed*, retrieved seeds from the garden of her deceased grandmother. Yet Lee Buttala says that the seeds were already in circulation, and the variety takes its name from an ice cream stand named for a cherished pet dog of the owners of Territorial Seed. Either way, the seed is now widely available, and well worth growing.

MELON: *Moon and Stars* (watermelon)

The seeds for Moon and Stars were first introduced in 1926 by Peter Henderson and Company, a seed catalog popular during that era. The melons range from 20 to 40 pounds, with a dark green rind decorated by golden-yellow "stars" and a few half-dollar–size moons. It is one of the most unusual heirloom watermelons, also known as Cherokee Moon and Stars, or Milky Way. It was almost lost completely until Kent Wheatley found it being grown by a farmer in Missouri and rescued seeds in 1981.

11

THE SELF-PRESERVATION GARDEN

PUTTING FOOD BY

DESIGN NOTES

This garden is based on the Victory Garden, where everything grown has a purpose. The results are skewed more toward nutrition and bounty than beauty and whimsy, yet for those who grow food for high productivity, this garden design will bring plenty of satisfaction. The maximum-yield varieties are good for fresh eating as well as for preserving in a root cellar.

INSPIRATION

In 1943, labor and transportation shortages brought on by World War II forced home gardeners to grow their own fruits and vegetables, and neighbors formed cooperatives and pooled their food resources. Gardeners plowed up their front yards, back lawns, and flower gardens to grow food, selecting vegetables that they could contribute to a public food supply. The result of this national effort was nearly twenty million Americans who planted a garden to feed their families and communities.

Many Americans also learned the mechanics and techniques of food preservation, the mainstay of most farm families, yet even suburban families were building root cellars and filling canning jars with beans, beets, cabbage, and peaches. The government printed posters promoting the health benefits of growing fresh vegetables and distributed plans for Victory Gardens. During this time of war, tending a 25×25-foot garden plot was part of daily life and considered a public duty and a way to contribute to the national efforts.

Becoming more self-sufficient starts by selecting the right vegetables: the ideal parsnip and carrot for storing in the root cellar, the largest beet for pickling, and the best cabbage for sauerkraut.

THE SELF-PRESERVATION GARDEN

DESIGN WISDOM
TIPS FOR GROWING

EMBRACE THE SEASONS
Extend the harvest by getting to know which crops prefer the cool of spring and fall or thrive in the heat of summer.

COMPOST HAPPENS
Build a compost pile near the garden. Keep it healthy and properly aerated, and alternate the colors by layering greens (grass and plants) and browns (leaves).

SOW COVER CROPS
Add organic matter and plant cover crops, which are plants grown solely to reinvigorate the soil during times when you are not growing food or flowers.

HARVEST CROPS OFTEN
Vegetables that grow too large will become inedible and drain energy from potential new growth. Keep the garden harvested frequently, and it will stay productive.

MANAGE THE WEEDS
If you pull weeds when they are small and before their seeds scatter, your weeding time will be greatly reduced. Get down on your knees and pull the weeds up at their roots. Leave them in the sun to dry out and wither before composting.

NEVER TOO THIN
Plants are more likely to succumb to pests or disease if they are planted too closely together. Thin the rows to allow enough space in between each plant to grow successfully.

GET TO KNOW YOUR SOIL
Soils differ widely, even in a single garden plot. A soil test from the local cooperative extension will help determine soil type and what you might need for amendments.

ADD A ROOT CELLAR
An ideal way to store food over the winter is in a root cellar, a cool room, an unheated basement, or a small house built into the ground so the crop doesn't freeze.

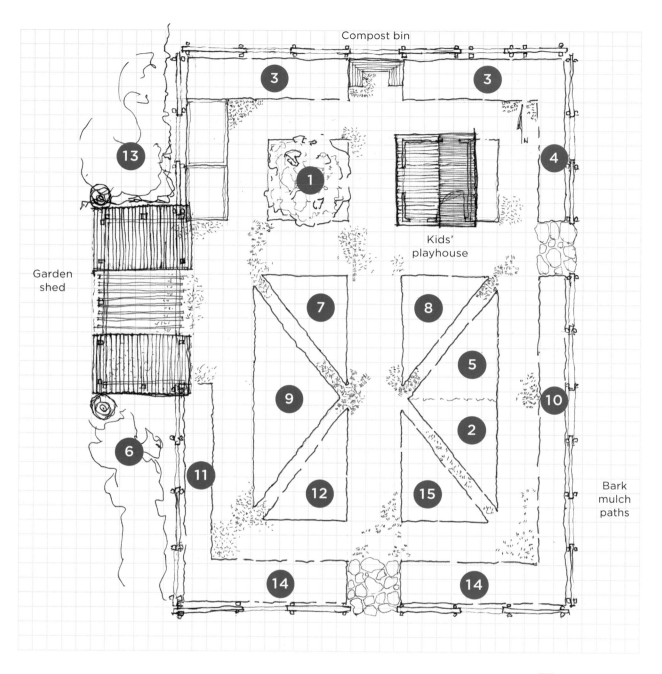

Compost bin

Garden shed

Kids' playhouse

Bark mulch paths

PLANT KEY

□ = 1 square foot

1. **APPLE:** Cox's Orange Pippin
2. **BEET:** Detroit Dark Red
3. **BLUEBERRY:** *Vaccinium corymbosum* Eliot (Northern) or Sunshine Blue (Southern)
4. **CABBAGE:** Early Jersey Wakefield
5. **CARROT:** Amarillo and Chantenay Red Core
6. **FLOWER:** Hollyhocks *Alcea ficifolis*
7. **HERB:** Parsley

8. **KOHLRABI:** Early Vienna
9. **LETTUCE:** Black Seeded Simpson
10. **LIMA BEAN:** King of the Garden
11. **ONION:** Wethersfield Red
12. **PARSNIP:** Hollow Crown
13. **RASPBERRY:** Heritage Fall Bearing
14. **SQUASH:** Blue Hubbard
15. **TURNIP:** Purple Top White Globe

SEED TALK

SOUTHERN HEIRLOOM FAVORITES GARDENER IRA WALLACE

The Southern Exposure Seed Exchange (SESE) is a cooperatively managed small heirloom seed catalog specializing in southeastern varieties, and a leading resource for gardeners south of the Mason-Dixon Line. Ira Wallace has been growing food since childhood, and when she moved to the Acorn Community Farm, she started to save the seeds from the garden. She especially loves the stories behind them, which she feels help keep seeds alive. She serves on the boards of the Organic Seed Alliance and the Organic Seed Growers and Trade Association, and in 2007, she founded the Harvest Festival at Thomas Jefferson's Monticello as a way to bring seed savers together to share, and as a public advocacy and educational event.

What is unique about the Southern Exposure Seed Exchange?

We are cooperatively owned and managed and only offer organic, heirloom, and open-pollinated varieties specific to the mid-Atlantic region. We have a large collection of specialty family heirlooms that are sent to us from gardeners in every state. We have cold seed storage to maintain 1,500 varieties of seed for the long term, and we currently offer 800 varieties online and 600 varieties in the catalog.

Is your interest in heirlooms for food or diversity?

Both, because I am a person who loves to eat, and I'm particularly interested in old flavor combinations that don't need so much sugar and fat to taste good. When I go for better flavor in a variety, it helps me eat better.

What is your current obsession?

I recently visited a farm that grew over ninety different varieties of collard greens. It was such a discovery to walk through the trial fields and see fields of purple and green leaves, flat and curly, large and small, tender and thick. Growing up in Florida, I always thought that collard greens needed to be cooked for a long time, but when the leaves are picked small and the ribs are removed, collards can be sautéed in garlic and olive oil for less than ten minutes.

Do you have favorite heirlooms?

In my garden, you'll always find Cajun Jewel okra; greasy pole beans, called "greasy" because they have no surface hairs, which makes them shiny; Grandma Nellie's Yellow Mushroom bush beans, which don't taste like mushrooms; Alabama blue collards; Early Jersey Wakefield cabbage, because I like to make slaw and kraut; and White Heron cucumbers, because the thin skin makes them tender for pickles.

For flowers, I grow Thai Red Roselle hibiscus; when dried, the red calyxes—not the flowers—have a sweet-tart flavor and make a bright red jam. Also old-fashioned vining petunias that will grow long into the fall and provide a color range, from white to pink and into a few dark purples.

Should everyone grow heirlooms and save seeds?

We live in a time of climate change, and heirlooms have been selected for resilience. We don't actually know what the future holds for us in terms of climate conditions. We have these varieties that have excellent flavor and wider disease resistance or the ability to deal with drought. Keeping that wide range of genetics available is like an ace in the hole for dealing with what Mother Nature and our own foolishness bring.

12

THE SHAKER GARDEN

HEALING HERBS AND FLOWERS

DESIGN NOTES

Eating involves all the senses, yet the first bite is taken with the eyes. Herbs and edible flowers have long been partners in the garden, and in the herbalist tradition, they are also ready to be a powerful teacher, guiding the gardener. Learn how to bring balance to body, mind, and spirit with herbs and flowers.

INSPIRATION

During the 1800s the Shaker community was largely responsible for growing the medicinal herbs and flowers used by physicians until modern medicine was invented. The Shakers were the first to sell herbs and flowers for use as a prevention rather than a treatment. Oils, salves, tinctures, and creams were made from flowers and herbs growing in their gardens; the Shakers were social pioneers, inventors, and craftspeople dedicated to self-sufficiency.

They were also the first to sell seeds for profit, due to a clever invention by Ebenezer Alden, who developed a printing press that would print paper envelopes for seeds and also wrote a growing guide titled *The Gardener's Manual*, which sold for six cents. Both proved popular and supported the Shaker communities.

Designing and planting a garden to be a pharmacy, and not just a show-place, requires allowing some of the plants to go to seed. In this design, the plants are packed together more snugly than usual, in waves of color ribbons. Remember that infusions made with herbs and edible flowers are gentle and taken over time; they are meant to be a supplement to and not a substitute for modern medicine for more serious illness.

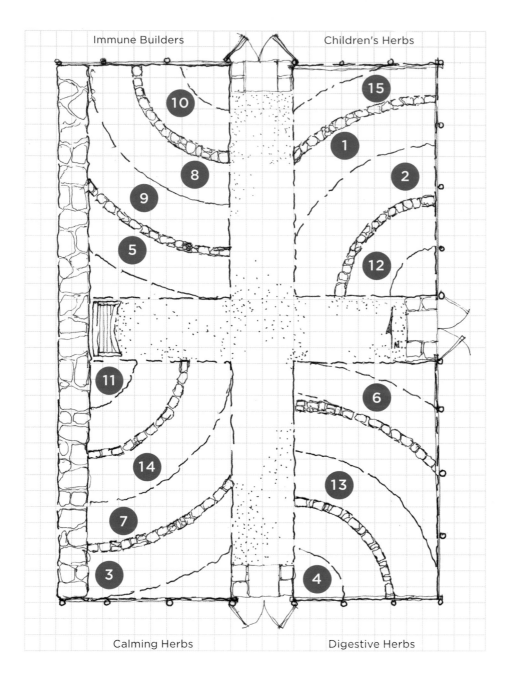

Immune Builders

Children's Herbs

Calming Herbs

Digestive Herbs

PLANT KEY

☐ = 1 square foot

1. **BORAGE**: *Borago officinalis*
2. **CALENDULA**: *Calendula officinalis*
3. **CATNIP**: *Nepeta cataria*
4. **CHAMOMILE**: *Matricaria recutita*
5. **ECHINACEA**: *Echinacea purpurea*
6. **FENNEL**: *Foeniculum vulgare*
7. **FEVERFEW**: *Tanacetum parthenium*
8. **GARLIC**: *Allium sativum*

9. **GINGER ROOT**: *Zingiber officinale*
10. **HORSERADISH**: *Armoracia rusticana*
11. **LAVENDER**: *Lavandula angustifolia* Munstead
12. **LEMON BALM**: *Melissa officinalis*
13. **MINT**: *Mentha spicata*
14. **OAT**: *Avena sativa*
15. **RED CLOVER**: *Trifolium pratense*

THE SHAKER GARDEN

DESIGN WISDOM
TIPS FOR GROWING

BUY PLANTS VERSUS SEEDS

Herb seeds are slow to germinate, so be patient when sowing and start them indoors, or seek a reliable source for herb plants.

KEEP A JOURNAL

Good record-keeping from season to season can provide clues to better understanding each plant. Learn which parts of the plant are harvested—flowers, leaves, or roots.

RELIABLE RESOURCES

Follow a trusted recipe when making tinctures, salves, and lotions, with the understanding that variations will exist between the plants. Most medicinal herbs should be harvested and dried before being added to other ingredients.

TAKE A CLASS

Study with an herbalist to learn firsthand professional knowledge about growing and using herbs. Take a series of classes, to accurately identify plants and how to work with them to make products.

GO ORGANIC

Learn to garden organically, because what touches your plants ultimately makes its way to you. Nourish your plants with a foliar seaweed spray instead of chemical fertilizer.

FERTILIZER-FREE

Most plants prefer rich soil, yet herbs benefit from just the opposite. Overfeeding the soil will generate long, lanky plants with less flavor and lower essential oils. Depriving herbs—just a bit—produces stronger essential properties.

LIVING HISTORY

Plants are no longer revered as a source of healing and prevention, yet modern medicine is still mostly derived from natural plant sources. Pick a plant and get to know the story of how it has been used throughout history.

MAKE A TOPIARY

Clip herbs into shapes, called topiaries. Start with the simplest shapes—balls, cones, pom-poms, or spirals—and grow them on frames.

SEED TALK

SLOW FOOD GARDENER FELDER RUSHING

Felder Rushing is a tenth-generation Mississippian and garden journalist who approaches gardening with a sense of whimsy. He has authored several books, including *Passalong Plants* and *Slow Gardening: A No-Stress Philosophy for All Senses and All Seasons*, and his message is simple: focus on finding and following personal bliss—through plants and creating gardens anywhere.

He lives part-time in a small cabin in Mississippi surrounded by gardens, and part-time in England, cultivating a huge variety of weather-hardy edible and ornamental plants. His signature style is to insert vernacular folk and yard art into the garden. This includes tire planters, bottle trees, and birdhouses made from old cowboy boots. He is most proud of what he grows in the back of his pickup truck: tomatoes, peppers, herbs, and okra. For the past twenty years, he has driven thousands of miles with all this food growing in the open bed. "I like to show people that you can grow food anywhere," he says.

How did you get started as a gardener?
My great-grandmother was born in 1880, and she was a serious horticulturist. She had 350 cultivars and a good knowledge of plants. She was also a good shot and ate squirrels. I spent a lot of time following her around, and she called me "the little professor" because I loved to learn from her. My grandmother—her daughter—grew only zinnias in a concrete container garden near the chicken yard, but she loved them as if they were prized roses. My own first garden was a cactus in a pot. Cactuses are weird, and you have to really love them, but they don't need much care.

How are pass-along plants and heirlooms similar?
Everyone has a plant they got from an Aunt Mamie or a friend. It might be a potted houseplant or an orange daylily. But this plant is something that reminds you of her, and it keeps the connection going. Not every pass-along plant is an heirloom, but it is something that is passed to one person and then to another and generally has a story, and typically it's been around a long time. Modern plants can become heirlooms. It does not have to be an old plant to be a pass-along or heirloom, just something that is meaningful and creates a connection to the past.

What do you recommend as a way to get started with a garden?
Aromatic culinary herbs are the best way to get new gardeners interested, because it gives them an instant edible plant that can be added to recipes and makes them feel good about growing something they did not have to buy. It gives them something to show off, too, and then once they have success with a container, it can spill over to flower and food beds later.

What are your favorite heirlooms for the South?
If it were up to the big-box stores, all the old varieties would disappear. Some heirlooms don't grow as well in the South because we have pests and diseases and heat. Sometimes we choose hybrids, but it is important to grow heirlooms to keep seeds growing.

Some of my favorites include Moon and Stars watermelon; Burgundy okra, which I grow for the flowers and the fruits; and Nancy Hall sweet potato, which can be grown in pots and planters as an ornamental. Pequin (bird's-eye) hot pepper is a historic heirloom. Georgia or Yates collards are both hearty and long-lasting in the garden. I always recommend common orange daylilies, because they grow all over the world in every type of soil. The buds are delicious cooked in butter.

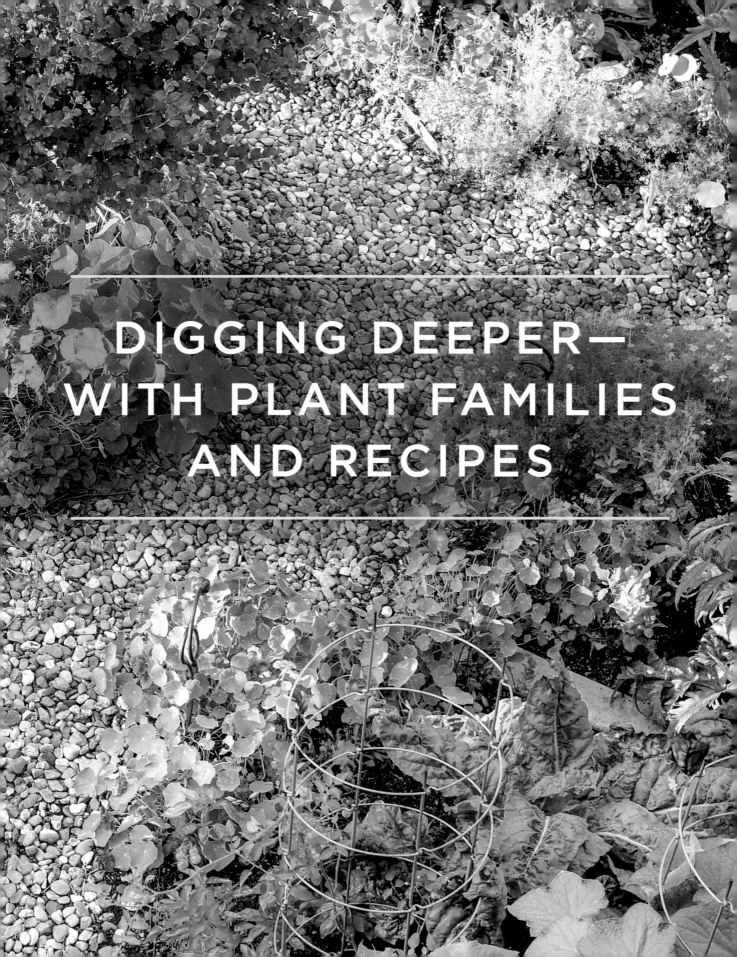

DIGGING DEEPER—
WITH PLANT FAMILIES
AND RECIPES

WITHOUT THE GREEN WORLD, the rest of the world would be quite different. We are here because of plants. It's that simple. Each of us depends on plants for air, food, and clothing, and in our gardens, plants surround us with beauty, fragrance, and wonder. We've been living together since the dawn of the human species, yet we still have a lot to learn about the structure of the plant world and how it works to keep us healthy.

The domesticated plants we cultivate in our gardens originated from a wild form; the DNA goes back further than that of the human species. You don't have to be a botanist or a scientist to dig just a little deeper into this web of life to discover how plants are grouped by plant families and then classified by genus, species, and varieties or cultivars. This basic classification is often noticeable by common shared characteristics, yet sometimes it is hard to find similarities.

Each plant is identified by binomial nomenclature, which is a scientific naming of plants established to create a more consistent and formal system that could be used universally. Developed by the Swedish botanist Carl Linnaeus in 1753, this method outlines the importance of providing the genus, species, and variety of every plant as a way to create a uniform way for gardeners and botanists to share mutual discoveries and cross-reference information.

To say two plants are in the same family is not to say they are the same, yet they may share similar characteristics. It's a way to help gardeners make sense of the plant world, and in this book and this chapter, it provides a glimpse into how heirlooms evolved; what basic elements from each plant have been bred and enhanced to make them more durable, more nutritious, more beautiful, and more disease resistant; and ultimately how to start your seeds, how to grow them in the garden, and what you need to know about saving the seeds.

Learning to group plants into their families and genera necessitates learning a little Latin to help keep everything straight. Knowing more about how to identify a plant's characteristics based on anatomical features—which might be the way they grow, the type of flowers, the shape of the stem, or the leaf structure, and whether they are annual, biennial, or perennial—is a way to dig even deeper. Thinking in terms of plant families, instead of just plants, will help you to become a better gardener.

Plants are like (most) people: they enjoy the company of other "like" plants, and this can be a way to provide companion planting, grouping similar plants in the garden together or setting up complementary groupings. And because often what grows together goes together at the table, you will become aware of options that can be used when substituting ingredients in recipes.

In the following plant section, you'll find an overview of eleven major plant families, with some favorite heirloom varieties listed. Keep in mind that there are far more heirloom varieties than what are included here. Seek out your own sources from seed libraries, seed exchanges, friends, and neighbors. Research alternative seed companies and support the small, diversified farms that embrace growing open-pollinated varieties and heirlooms to infuse the seed industry with new vigor and intention.

SEED SUPPLIERS AND BREEDERS

Here's a short list of sources for purchasing the organic, open-pollinated, and heirloom seeds mentioned in this book.

Adaptive Seeds	Peace Seedlings	Siskiyou Seeds
Experimental Farm Network	Peaceful Valley Farm Supply	Southern Exposure Seed
Fedco Seeds	Ronnigers Potatoes	Exchange
Filaree Garlic Farm	Prairie Road Organic Seed	Sow True Seed
Fruition Seeds	Row 7 Seeds	Sustainable Seed Co.
High Mowing Organic Seeds	Sand Hill Preservation Center	True Love Seeds
Hudson Valley Seed	Seed Savers Exchange	Turtle Seed
JL Hudson, Seedsman	Seeds from Italy	Uprising Seeds
Kitazawa Seed Company	Select Seeds / Antique Flowers	Victory Seeds
Native Seeds/Search	Sierra Seeds	Wild Garden Seeds

THE AMARANTH FAMILY

Amaranthaceae (formerly Chenopodiaceae)

EDIBLE SPECIES:
amaranth, beet, chard, lamb's-quarter, orache, quinoa, spinach

The amaranth (or goosefoot) family contains over 2,500 species. Most are annuals (i.e., they grow for only one season and then set seed), a few are perennials (i.e., they will grow for many years and set seed in the second year), and some are trees and vines. Distinguishable traits include large, edible, flat leaves that are exceptionally high in proteins. In the case of quinoa, amaranth, and red Aztec spinach, the flowers evolve into a seed head with dramatic spikes or panicles, which are harvested as a grain. Several species, such as purslane and lamb's-quarter, are considered weedy and invasive.

ROASTED BALSAMIC BEET AND WALNUT SALAD SERVES 4 TO 6

Italian heirloom Chioggia beets are ideal in salads that show off the concentric candylike stripes, yet any good beet will do for this recipe. Roasting the beets in balsamic vinegar brings out an extra-deep, rich flavor.

¾ cup extra-virgin olive oil, plus more for the dish

½ cup plus 2 tablespoons balsamic vinegar

2 tablespoons finely chopped shallot or red onion

½ teaspoon Dijon mustard

6 medium beets (about 2 pounds), preferably Chioggia, greens removed

1 tablespoon pure maple syrup

½ teaspoon sea salt, plus more to taste

¼ teaspoon freshly ground black pepper, plus more to taste

2 tart heirloom apples (such as Baldwin or Macintosh), peeled, cored, and cut into ½-inch cubes

1 small red onion, thinly sliced

½ cup walnut pieces, coarsely chopped and toasted

½ cup crumbled feta cheese

½ cup chopped fresh Italian flat-leaf parsley

To make the dressing, in a small jar with a lid, combine ½ cup of the oil, ¼ cup of the vinegar, the shallot, and mustard. Shake vigorously to blend. Set aside.

Preheat the oven to 400°F. Lightly oil a 9 × 12-inch baking dish.

Scrub the beets and trim the stem ends to 1 inch; keep the root ends and peels intact. Toss the beets with 2 tablespoons of the oil, place them in the prepared baking dish, and cover with foil or an ovenproof lid. Bake until the beets are tender all the way through, about 45 minutes; insert a sharp knife in the beets to test for doneness.

Remove the dish from the oven, but do not turn it off. Cool the beets slightly, rub off their skins, and slice the beets into quarters. Return the quartered beets to the baking dish, allowing some room between each. In a small bowl, blend ¼ cup of the vinegar, the maple syrup, and the remaining 2 tablespoons oil, then drizzle over the beets; sprinkle with the salt and pepper. Cover the dish and return to the oven.

Roast the beets for another 15 minutes. Remove from the oven and add the remaining 2 tablespoons vinegar. Carefully toss the beets to coat, then roast, uncovered, until fork-tender, about 10 minutes more.

Cut the beets into ½-inch cubes, or slice and place them in a salad bowl. Add the apples, onion, walnuts, feta, and parsley, and toss gently. Mix as much dressing as you like into the salad, generally 1 to 2 tablespoons per person. Season with salt and pepper to taste. Any remaining dressing can be refrigerated for several weeks.

RAINBOW BEET SPOONBREAD

SERVES 4 TO 6

Spoonbreads are an elegant way to serve beets: their red juices bleed into the yellow soufflé to create an unusual rainbow effect. Farm-raised eggs make all the difference in flavor and color in this soufflé.

2 medium beets,
preferably Detroit Red

2 tablespoons
extra-virgin olive oil,
plus more for the pan

¼ cup Cointreau or other
sweet fruity liqueur

Zest and juice of 1 lemon

1 teaspoon sugar

½ teaspoon freshly ground
coarse sea salt

¼ teaspoon freshly ground
black pepper

4 tablespoons (½ stick)
unsalted butter

2 tablespoons grated
Parmigiano-Reggiano cheese

½ cup crumbled
soft chèvre goat cheese

3 tablespoons
all-purpose flour

1 cup half-and-half

½ cup finely chopped
steamed beet greens

4 large eggs, separated,
at room temperature

Position a rack in the center of the oven. Preheat the oven to 400°F. Scrub the beets and trim the stem ends to 1 inch; keep the root ends and peels intact. Toss the beets with the olive oil, place in a lightly oiled baking pan, and cover with foil or an ovenproof lid. Bake until the beets are tender all the way through, about 45 minutes; insert a sharp knife in the beets to test for doneness.

Cool the beets slightly, rub off their skins, and thinly slice the beets or chop them into 1-inch cubes; there should be about 2 cups. Transfer the beets to a medium bowl and add the Cointreau, lemon zest and juice, sugar, salt, and pepper.

Butter the inside of a 9 × 12-inch baking dish or 8-inch-round soufflé dish with 1 tablespoon of the butter. Sprinkle the bottom of the dish with the Parmigiano-Reggiano, then lay the beets evenly on the bottom of the dish, reserving the liquid, and crumble on the goat cheese.

Prepare a béchamel sauce by gently melting the remaining 3 tablespoons butter in a medium saucepan over medium-low heat. Slowly whisk in the flour, stirring continuously, and let the mixture gently bubble without browning for a few minutes. Gradually add the half-and-half, whisking constantly until thickened. Stir in the beet greens. Remove the pan from the heat and cool slightly. Whisk the egg yolks, one at a time, into the cooled béchamel sauce.

Place the egg whites in a medium bowl or the bowl of a stand mixer fitted with the whisk attachment. Beat the egg whites until they form soft stiff peaks, about 5 minutes. Fold the egg whites into the béchamel sauce, then gently pour the sauce over the beets, and smooth the top. Place the dish in the oven and bake until puffed and golden brown, about 30 minutes. Serve immediately.

BORSCHT *with Beef* SERVES 6

A visual treat in winter: the red beet broth is accented with a plop of white crème fraîche and garnished with tiny green specks of fresh dill. Make it a day before serving for the best flavor, then dig in with a big spoon and a side of hearty sourdough bread.

2 tablespoons extra-virgin olive oil

1 large onion, coarsely chopped

2 large garlic cloves, coarsely chopped

1 teaspoon caraway seeds

4 or 5 medium beets, preferably Improved Crosby Egyptian, greens removed

1 quart homemade canned tomatoes, or 1 (28-ounce) can chopped tomatoes

1 teaspoon dried dill

½ teaspoon ground cumin

1 pound pasture-raised ground beef

1 teaspoon coarse sea salt, plus more to taste

½ teaspoon freshly ground black pepper, or to taste

2 tablespoons apple cider vinegar

1 cup crème fraîche or whole-milk yogurt

Fresh dill or parsley, finely chopped, for garnish

In a 4-quart stockpot, heat the oil over medium heat. Reduce the heat to low, add the onion and garlic, and sauté until soft, 5 to 8 minutes. Add the caraway and stir to blend.

Scrub and trim the beets, peeling away any rough spots, and cut them into quarters. In a food processor fitted with a grating blade, push the beets through to shred them into small bits; there should be about 6 cups. Stir the grated beets into the stockpot.

Pour in the tomatoes, dried dill, cumin, and enough water to cover the beets by at least 1 inch, 3 to 4 cups. Cover, bring to a low boil, and simmer until the beets are soft when pierced with a knife, 15 to 20 minutes.

While the soup simmers, heat a medium skillet over medium heat. Add the ground beef and sauté for 5 minutes until lightly browned, breaking it into smaller pieces with a wooden spoon. Season with the salt and pepper. Using a slotted spoon, transfer the meat to the stockpot, leaving any fat behind in the pan. Stir the vinegar into the stockpot, simmer for another 10 minutes, and add salt to taste. Serve in bowls with a dollop of crème fraîche and a sprinkle of fresh dill.

COLLARD GREENS AND SAUSAGE SOUP SERVES 6 TO 8

Prepare collard greens by stacking the leaves on top of each other, rolling them into a tube, and then slicing them crosswise into thin strips to add to this hearty soup.

¼ cup extra-virgin olive oil

2 hot Italian sausages, cut into ½-inch pieces

2 sweet Italian sausages, cut into ½-inch pieces

1 onion, finely chopped (about 1 cup)

4 garlic cloves, minced

¼ teaspoon crushed red pepper flakes

Salt and freshly ground black pepper

2 pounds Yukon Gold potatoes (6 to 8), peeled and cut into ¾-inch pieces

4 cups chicken broth

1 pound collard greens, stacked and sliced into fine strips (about 6 cups)

Heat 1 tablespoon of the oil in an 8-quart stockpot over medium-high heat until shimmering. Add the sausages and cook, stirring occasionally, until lightly browned, 4 to 5 minutes. Using a slotted spoon, transfer the sausage to a bowl and set aside.

Reduce the heat to medium and add the onion, garlic, and red pepper flakes. Season with a generous sprinkling of salt and black pepper to taste. Cook, stirring frequently, until the onion is translucent, 3 to 5 minutes. Add the potatoes, broth, and 4 cups water and bring to a boil. Reduce the heat and simmer, uncovered, until the potatoes are just tender, about 10 minutes.

With a measuring cup or soup ladle, transfer 1 cup of the vegetable solids and 1 cup of the broth to a blender. Add the remaining 3 tablespoons oil to the blender and process until very smooth and well blended, about 1 minute. Set aside.

Add the collard greens to the stockpot and simmer for 5 minutes. Add the reserved sausages and continue to simmer until the greens are tender, 8 to 10 minutes longer.

Stir the pureed soup mixture from the blender back into the stockpot, bring back to a simmer, and serve hot.

SAUTÉED CHARD *with Ginger* SERVES 4

If you have been holding onto a treasured bottle of aged Italian balsamic vinegar, it's time to add a few drops at the end of this recipe. A little bit goes a long way, so adjust accordingly.

1 large bunch chard, preferably Rainbow (about 1 pound)

1 tablespoon plus ½ teaspoon sea salt

2 tablespoons extra-virgin olive oil

2 garlic cloves, smashed and finely minced

1 (2-inch) knob of fresh ginger, peeled and thinly sliced

1 hot pepper, preferably Long Red Cayenne

¼ teaspoon freshly ground black pepper

2 tablespoons unsalted butter

1 to 2 tablespoons balsamic vinegar

Separate the chard leaves from the stems. Cut the stems in half lengthwise and slice them very thinly crosswise. Stack the leaves in batches, roll them up, and cut them into thin strips (or chiffonade).

Fill a medium saucepan with 2 inches of water and bring it to a boil. Add 1 tablespoon of the salt, drop in the leaves and stems, and blanch them just until wilted, about 2 minutes. Drain and gently squeeze out the excess water.

In a large sauté pan, heat the oil over medium heat. Reduce the heat to low, add the garlic, ginger, and hot pepper and cook until soft and lightly golden, about 10 minutes. Add the chard, the remaining teaspoon salt, and the black pepper. Cook until tender, about 5 minutes. Remove from the heat, add the butter, and swirl to melt.

Divide the chard among 4 salad plates, drizzle each with a touch of vinegar, and serve.

HEIRLOOM CULTIVARS IN THE AMARANTH FAMILY

AMARANTH: *Elena's Rojo, Green Callaloo, Hopi Red Dye, love-lies-bleeding, Molten Fire*

BEET: *Bull's Blood, McGregor's Favorite, Lutz Green Leaf, Early Blood Turnip, Albino, Golden, Chioggia, Formonova, Crosby's Improved Egyptian, Detroit Dark Red, Cylindra*

CHARD: *Perpetual Spinach, Sea Kale, Five Color Silverbeet, Bionda di Lyon, Fordhook Giant*

SPINACH: *Galilee, Amsterdam Prickly Seeded, Giant Noble, Bloomsdale Long Standing, Merlo Nero, Monstrueux de Viroflay*

SPINACH AND CHEESE CUSTARD

SERVES 4

The leaves of Malabar spinach are more succulent than those of traditional spinach, and the variety makes a lovely ornamental vine. Try it in this recipe, or use a more traditional heirloom spinach such as Bloomsdale Long Standing.

1 tablespoon unsalted butter, softened

¼ teaspoon sea salt, plus more for the pot

3 cups fresh spinach leaves, preferably Malabar or Bloomsdale Long Standing, well rinsed

1 cup heavy cream

4 large egg yolks

½ cup shredded sharp Cheddar cheese

½ cup shredded Gruyère cheese

⅛ teaspoon freshly ground black pepper

⅛ teaspoon freshly grated nutmeg

Preheat the oven to 325°F. Generously butter four 8-ounce ramekins.

Bring a large pot of salted water to a boil. Add the spinach and cook just until tender, about 3 minutes. Drain and rinse the spinach under cold water. When it's cool enough to handle, squeeze out the excess moisture a handful at a time, and chop coarsely. You should have about 1 cup chopped spinach.

In a medium bowl, whisk together the cream and egg yolks until well combined. Stir in the cooked spinach, cheeses, ½ teaspoon salt, pepper, and nutmeg. Ladle or pour equal quantities of the custard into the prepared ramekins and place them in a roasting pan.

Add enough hot water to the roasting pan to come halfway up the sides of the ramekins. Carefully transfer the pan to the oven and bake until the custard is set when given a slight shake or when a sharp knife inserted comes out clean, about 35 minutes. Remove the ramekins from the roasting pan and let stand for 5 minutes. Run a knife around the inside of each ramekin and invert on separate plates to unmold. Serve hot.

MEET THE AMARANTH FAMILY

BEET GREENS

Most beets are grown primarily for their roots yet can also be harvested for the leaves. The brilliant crimson-green foliage is tender when harvested young, and as long as some leaves are left on the plant, the roots will continue to develop. Rich in flavor and high in nutrition, beet greens are ideal for a summer salad mix with dramatic burgundy-colored leaves.

BEETS

Beets are a common root vegetable grown by most gardeners, yet the Chioggia is a sweet Italian heirloom variety known for the decorative interior also known as "candy stripe." Harvest beets when the shoulders start to emerge from the soil; do not leave them in the ground too long or they will become woody.

CHARD

Chard was known in colonial Virginia as "poor man's greens" because it grew with wild abandon in every garden. Available in a variety of colors ranging from crimson red to pink, yellow, and white, chard is still a favorite among gardeners. In the 1920s, the W. Atlee Burpee Company catalog introduced Fordhook Giant, with large green leaves and a prominent white rib; it was named after Fordhook Farm, where the seed catalog began in the late 1800s.

GOOD-KING-HENRY
(Chenopodium bonus-henricus)

For hundreds of years, Good-King-Henry, also known as Lincolnshire spinach or "fat hen" (because chickens adore this green), was grown as a common potherb in vegetable gardens. Now either forgotten or considered a weed, it is still worthwhile to try, mostly because it is a perennial salad green. The small triangular leaves taste similar to chard or spinach; a little dry when eaten raw, it's best cooked or blended with other greens.

THE CABBAGE FAMILY

Brassicaceae or Cruciferae

EDIBLE SPECIES: *arugula, broccoli, Brussels sprouts, cabbage, cauliflower, collards, kale, kohlrabi, nasturtium, radish, turnip*

Cabbage, broccoli, cauliflower, Brussels sprouts, and kohlrabi, as well as leafy kale, collards, and spicy radishes, are all part of this family of cold-hardy vegetables. Also included in the mix are wild greens, including arugula, mustard, tatsoi, and watercress. All the crops in this large family contain a strong- and often bitter-tasting quality due to a compound called glucosinolate, which contains the health benefits associated with the whole crucifer group. In northern climates, after the first frost, a cold snap turns the bitterness into sweetness.

The key to success in growing this family of plants is to feed them regularly during the growing season with an organic seaweed fertilizer and a side dressing of compost.

PUREED GILFEATHER TURNIP
with Apples   SERVES 4

In Vermont, it is not Thanksgiving without a bowl of turnips. Gilfeather turnips, actually part rutabaga, and named by the Vermont family who has handed the variety down through several generations, are the biggest and best available. Yet no matter what variety you use, this easy dish is a wonderful addition to the table.

1 large heirloom turnip, preferably Gilfeather, peeled and cut into 1½-inch chunks

1 tablespoon unsalted butter, plus more as needed

2 large tart apples, preferably Macintosh (about 1 pound), peeled, cored, and cut into 1-inch cubes

½ teaspoon freshly grated nutmeg or ground cinnamon

Place a collapsible vegetable steamer in a large saucepan and add enough cold water to reach the bottom of the steamer. Add the turnip, cover the pan tightly, and bring the water to a boil over high heat. Reduce the heat to medium and cook until the turnip is very tender, about 30 minutes. Transfer to a food processor and puree.

Meanwhile, melt the butter in a large skillet over medium-high heat. Add the apples and cook, stirring occasionally, until golden brown and tender, about 5 minutes. Add the turnip puree and the nutmeg and mix well. Serve hot with more butter, if desired.

SAUTÉED KOHLRABI *in Savory Cream*

SERVES 4

This simple and savory recipe features a little-known vegetable yet will quickly become one of your new favorites. Seasoned with fresh summer savory, this creamy side dish is a winner.

Prepare kohlrabi by peeling the outside, coarsely grating or finely dicing the flesh, and tossing it with a bit of salt to release the moisture before cooking. Sautéed in butter and finished with cream, kohlrabi makes a win-win savory side dish to serve in late fall.

2 large heirloom green or purple kohlrabi (about 1 pound)

1 teaspoon coarse sea salt, plus more as needed

4 tablespoons (½ stick) unsalted butter

1 medium yellow or red onion, thinly sliced

3 tablespoons heavy cream or half-and-half

1 tablespoon finely chopped fresh summer savory or thyme, plus fresh sprigs for garnish

Freshly ground black pepper to taste

With a paring knife, remove the top and root ends from each kohlrabi, chopping and reserving any young and tender leaves. Gently peel off the tough outer skin, which is thin yet fibrous. Grate both kohlrabi on the large holes of a box grater or in a food processer fitted with a grating disk; you should have about 4 cups.

Toss the kohlrabi in a colander with the sea salt and let it stand in the sink to drain for about 30 minutes. Rinse under cold water and gently squeeze out any excess liquid.

In a medium skillet over medium heat, melt the butter. Add the onions and sauté, stirring occasionally to keep them from sticking to the pan. Once they begin to turn lightly brown, add the kohlrabi and chopped leaves, if using, and cover. Cook the vegetables, stirring occasionally, for about 10 minutes. Uncover and continue to cook, stirring occasionally, until the edges of the kohlrabi turn golden brown, about 10 minutes.

Stir in the cream and the chopped herbs, and continue to cook until the cream is fully absorbed, about 3 minutes. Taste and season with salt and pepper. Serve hot, garnished with fresh herb sprigs.

HEIRLOOM CULTIVARS IN THE CABBAGE FAMILY

ARUGULA: *Sylvetta, Apollo, Enrico Rao*

BROCCOLI: *Romanesco, Calabrese, Early Purple Sprouting, Rapini, De Cicco*

CABBAGE: *Early Jersey Wakefield, Cour di Bue, Eersteling, Savoy, Kalibos, Filderkraut, Violaceo di Verona, Quintal d'Alsace, January King, Cannonball, Portuguese (Couve Tronchuda)*

CAULIFLOWER: *Green Macerata, Purple of Sicily, Snowball, Violetta Italia, Purple Cape*

COLLARDS: *Vates, Georgia Southern Creole, Cabbage, Ellen Felton Dark*

KALE: *Nero di Toscana (Lacinato or Blue Tuscan), Red Russian, Couve Galega, Ragged Jack, Siberian, Smooth German*

KOHLRABI: *Purple Vienna, White Vienna, Giant White, Blauer Speck*

RADISH: *Watermelon, China Rose, Chinese Green, 18 Day, Early Scarlet Globe, French Breakfast, Japanese Daikon, Munchener Bier, Singara Rat's Tail*

TURNIP: *Gilfeather, Boule d'Or, Purple Top White Globe, White Egg*

BRUSSELS SPROUT SLAW

with Cashew-Curry Dressing   SERVES 4

A favorite way to serve Brussels sprouts is steamed and topped with a knob of sweet butter and a crack of black pepper, yet this raw winter salad with a delicious vegan dressing has become a new rival.

4 cups Brussels sprouts (about 2 pounds), preferably Long Island Improved

2 large curly kale leaves, preferably Lacinato, finely chopped (about 2 cups)

½ small red onion, preferably Southport Red Globe, finely chopped

½ cup grated Parmigiano-Reggiano

½ cup chopped walnuts, lightly toasted in a dry skillet

⅓ cup dried currants

Cashew-Curry Dressing (recipe follows)

Trim the stems and outside leaves of the Brussels sprouts and coarsely chop them into ¼-inch pieces or, if you are comfortable with a mandoline, slice them into thin slivers. Transfer them to a salad bowl and add the kale, onion, cheese, walnuts, and currants.

Spoon all of the dressing over the vegetables and toss to coat. Refrigerate to keep cool until ready to serve.

CASHEW-CURRY DRESSING

Makes ½ cup

½ cup cashews

½ cup boiling water

¼ cup apple cider vinegar

1½ tablespoons lemon juice

1 tablespoon curry powder

2 teaspoons maple syrup

½ teaspoon sea salt, plus more as needed

In a small bowl, soak the cashews in the boiling water for 10 minutes; drain well. In a blender, combine the cashews, vinegar, lemon juice, curry powder, maple syrup, and salt, and puree on high speed until smooth, less than a minute. Transfer to a bowl until ready to use as a dressing for the salad. Refrigerate for up to a week.

BROCCOLI RAAB *Low and Slow* SERVES 4

Slightly bitter broccoli raab, also known as cima di rapa or rapini, might be too bitter for some palates, yet when it is cooked slowly over low heat for as long as possible, the flavor mellows. Serve this dish alone or over pasta topped with burrata, grated cheese, or a sprinkle of toasted bread crumbs; if any leftovers exist, fold them into an omelet the next day.

1 large bunch broccoli raab
(1 pound)

¼ cup plus 2 tablespoons
extra-virgin olive oil
(see Note)

3 garlic cloves,
finely chopped

½ teaspoon sea salt

¼ teaspoon freshly ground
black pepper

4 small burrata cheese balls,
or ¼ cup shaved
Parmigiano-Reggiano

⅛ cup good-quality
balsamic vinegar

Submerge the broccoli raab in cold water, lift it out, and set it into a colander. Let it almost drip dry, but not completely. Coarsely chop the stems and florets into 2-inch pieces.

Heat ¼ cup of the oil in a cast-iron pan over medium heat. Drop in the broccoli raab by the handful until the pan is full. Add the garlic, salt, and pepper, and give it a stir. The salt will draw the water from the greens, but go light on the seasoning so you can taste the raab.

Cover the pan and reduce the heat to very low. Cook, stirring occasionally, until the broccoli is reduced and tender, 20 to 30 minutes. Expect it to reduce to about a quarter of its original volume. Turn off the heat.

Distribute the raab between 4 plates. Top each with fresh burrata and evenly drizzle the remaining 2 tablespoons oil and some vinegar over the tops.

NOTE: Two tablespoons of the oil is drizzled on the cooked broccoli raab. You can use the same oil as you did for sautéing or break out a bottle of something especially nice.

ARUGULA, COUSCOUS, AND LENTIL SALAD *with Lemon Vinaigrette*

SERVES 4 TO 6

Grains and lentils amp up the protein base for a salad that can be made with an assortment of seasonal greens, such as kale, endive, or spinach.

1 cup tiny black or green dried French lentils

1 cup vegetable stock or water

1 cup whole-wheat couscous

Lemon Vinaigrette (recipe follows)

4 cups fresh arugula

1 small yellow onion or 6 scallions, coarsely chopped

1 pint cherry tomatoes, halved

1 English cucumber, peeled, seeded, and cut into ½-inch cubes

½ cup crumbled feta cheese

In a small saucepan, combine the lentils and enough water to cover by 1 inch; bring to a simmer over medium heat, about 15 minutes. Be careful not to overcook the lentils or they will fall apart in the salad. Drain any excess water and cool.

In a medium saucepan, bring the stock to a boil. Add the couscous, cover, remove from the heat, and leave until all the liquid has been absorbed, about 10 minutes.

In a large salad bowl, combine the cooked lentils and couscous, tossing while slightly warm with half the vinaigrette.

Finely chop the arugula and toss with the lentils and couscous, along with the onions, tomatoes, and cucumber. Sprinkle with the feta cheese and add as much of the remaining vinaigrette as desired. Toss gently to coat everything with the vinaigrette. Serve right away.

LEMON VINAIGRETTE
Makes ½ cup

¼ cup extra-virgin olive oil

Juice of 2 lemons

⅛ cup red wine vinegar

1 tablespoon Dijon mustard

2 garlic cloves, mashed

½ teaspoon sea salt

¼ teaspoon black pepper

In a small jar with a lid, combine the oil, lemon juice, vinegar, mustard, and garlic. Shake vigorously to blend. Add the salt and pepper, and shake again.

MEET THE CABBAGE FAMILY

ARUGULA

Arugula (also known as rocket) is a native of Europe, particularly the Mediterranean region. A piquant, peppery green, arugula is the superstar in most mesclun mixes because it grows rapidly and has an assertive flavor that can dominate a salad unless it is paired with milder greens. Sylvetta is the smallest and wildest version that will often reseed and return yearly.

BROCCOLI

Broccoli is common, yet a distinctive variety known as Romanesco is well worth growing. The conical florets grow into spirals, each bud composed of smaller buds in a Fibonacci series. Sometimes called Roman cauliflower, it is the result of selective breeding by Italian farmers in the sixteenth century.

BROCCOLI RAAB

As the Italian population grew in the United States, so did some of their beloved vegetables, and Italian or Calabrese Green Sprouting broccoli, or Cima de Rapa (broccoli raab), was introduced. An easier and more beautiful crop to grow than a traditional large-head variety, broccoli raab takes far less time for the first harvest to begin. Encourage productivity by consistently watering and using organic fertilizer.

CABBAGE

Short-stemmed, hardy cabbage is an old English standby, popular in kitchen gardens for centuries. Since it is widely available in stores, most gardeners don't grow it, yet it is one of the most beautiful plants in a garden. When cabbage arrives at the store, the outer leaves have been removed, since they add weight and take up space, yet the delight of watching the cabbage head grow, layer by layer, leaf by leaf, makes it a worthwhile effort.

COLLARD GREENS

Collards are hearty enough to withstand cool temperatures and sturdy enough to thrive in the heat, with cut-and-come-again qualities for harvests throughout the growing season. Collards have wide, flat leaves that can be picked when young for salad or sautéed when full size.

KALE

The wrinkled dark-green leaves of kale are well known, listed among Thomas Jefferson's favorites. The full-size plants can grow up to 3 feet tall, branching 2 feet wide, taking up a large space in a small garden. The Lacinato variety, also known as Blue Tuscan or dinosaur kale, has elongated ostrich-plumed narrow leaves that are tender and dramatic to grow in the garden.

MUSTARD

All mustard greens are hot and spicy, yet as the leaves grow larger, they become especially pungent. A wide variety of different mustard greens are available for the home garden, including mizuna, a narrow spear-shaped leaf with undulated edges; Purple Osaka; Red Giant, a rounder leaf mottled in a deep burgundy purple; and the common yellow mustard, grown for spicy leaves but mostly for the seed heads that are crushed for mustard seed.

SEA KALE
(Crambe maritima)

Native to Europe, sea kale was harvested in the wild for thousands of years before it was first cultivated for a home garden in the late 1600s. Sea kale takes up a wide berth in a garden, yet you might not know it when it first appears as a small sprout. The plant evolves into something quite substantial, with undulated gray-blue leaves and tall, billowing flowers.

TURNIP

The flat, round, smooth white roots of turnip mature just after radishes and are best harvested young in the spring or in the early fall after a frost. Sweet and crisp, turnips have the snap of radishes without the bite. Purple Top White Globe, once the prized staple of homestead gardens, is a traditional old-time variety.

THE CARROT FAMILY

Umbelliferae or Apiaceae

EDIBLE SPECIES:
anise, caraway, carrot, celeriac, celery, cilantro (coriander), dill, lovage, parsley, parsnip

Carrots, parsnips, celery, and celeriac (or celery root) are often placed together as a group of root vegetables; actually, they all belong to the Umbelliferae family, named for the umbrella- or fan-shaped flower that forms before the plants go to seed. This family of aromatic flowering plants contains more than 3,700 species, including some familiar culinary herbs. The tiny flowers in their "umbrellas" make fine nectar for ladybugs, parasitic wasps, and predatory flies, and the black swallowtail butterfly uses this plant family for food and as host plants. An heirloom that dates back many centuries, the carrot was originally purple but bred to be white, yellow, and, relatively recently, orange.

CELERY ROOT VICHYSSOISE SERVES 6

Celery root is the main ingredient in French rémoulade salad seasoned with fresh tarragon and creamy mayonnaise. Or try this smooth, refreshing soup, served either hot or cold.

2 medium leeks,
preferably King Richard
or Blue Solaise
(about 1 pound)

2 tablespoons (¼ stick)
unsalted butter

1 medium heirloom celery
root, preferably Giant Prague
(about 1 pound)

4 medium potatoes,
preferably German
Butterball or Early Rose
(about 1 pound),
scrubbed and diced
(about 2 cups)

½ teaspoon sea salt

¼ teaspoon freshly ground
black pepper

4 cups vegetable
or chicken stock,
preferably homemade

Zest and juice of 1 lemon

¼ cup heavy cream
or half-and-half,
for garnish

Chopped fresh parsley,
for garnish

To prepare the leeks, remove the tip of the root end and cut the tops off just above the dark green leaves. Slice the leeks in half lengthwise, open the layers, and place under running water to clean away soil or sand that can be in between the layers of the leaves. Slice the leeks into roughly ½-inch pieces; there should be about 4 cups.

In a 4-quart stockpot over medium heat, melt the butter. Add the leeks and sauté until softened, about 8 minutes.

Peel and quarter the celery root. Chop it into ½-inch cubes; there should be about 2 cups. Add the celery root, potatoes, salt, and pepper to the stockpot and give it a stir to combine. Slowly pour in the stock, cover, and reduce the heat to a simmer. Cook until the vegetables are soft, about 25 minutes. Remove from the heat. Add the lemon zest and 2 teaspoons of the lemon juice.

With an immersion blender, whir until silky smooth, a minute or two. If you don't have an immersion blender, carefully transfer the soup to a traditional blender, being careful not to overfill it. Cover and blend until silky smooth, with a kitchen towel on the cover to keep the hot soup contained, a minute or two. This may need to be done in several batches.

Ladle the soup into bowls, garnish with a swirl of heavy cream and some parsley, and serve hot or cold.

HEIRLOOM CULTIVARS IN THE CARROT FAMILY

CARROT: *Touchon, Scarlet Nantes, Chantenay Red Core, Danvers Half Long, Cosmic Purple, Kuroda, Purple Dragon, Paris Market, Long Red Surrey*

STALK CELERY: *Chinese White Celery, Tendercrisp, Utah Tall, Pink Plume*

CELERY ROOT: *Giant Prague, Bianco Verona Veneto*

LEAFY FENNEL: *Smokey Bronze*

FENNEL ROOT (FINOCCHIO): *Florence, Romanesco, Di Parma Sel, Prado, Montebianco*

PARSNIP: *Half Long Guernsey, Hollow Crown*

BRAISED COSMIC CARROTS

with Tarragon   SERVES 4

Carrots are at their best fresh, pulled straight from the ground, yet cooking them increases their nutritional content. Simmer carrots over low heat in a little water with a good knob of butter to keep all the color and nutrition in the same pot.

8 medium heirloom carrots
(about 1 pound),
preferably mixed colors

2 tablespoons (¼ stick)
unsalted butter,
plus more as needed

Sea salt and freshly ground
black pepper

1 tablespoon chopped
fresh tarragon

Trim the ferny green tops off the carrots (see Note), leaving 2 inches of stem and keeping the roots intact. If the carrots are young and tender, keep them whole; otherwise, cut them into matchsticks. Place the carrots in a 1-quart saucepan along with the butter and a tablespoon or two of water to barely cover.

Simmer the carrots over low heat until tender, about 15 minutes, adding more water or butter as needed to keep the carrots from sticking to the pan. Season lightly with salt and pepper, sprinkle with the tarragon, and serve.

NOTE: For a flavorful and crunchy garnish, chop the carrot tops into small pieces and fry in hot olive oil for a few seconds, until crisp. Remove to a paper towel–lined plate with a slotted spoon. Sprinkle salt over the carrot tops before serving.

ROASTED ROOT VEGETABLE PLATTER SERVES 4 TO 6

Root vegetables are especially delicious when roasted, and a snap to prepare. Dress lightly with olive oil, stick in a slow oven, and head out to the garden to weed for an hour while they roast. Serve this us a side with a nice homemade pasta or pumpkin ravioli.

½ cup extra-virgin olive oil

6 assorted small heirloom potatoes, preferably Rose Red Finn, scrubbed

4 carrots, scrubbed and cut into matchsticks

2 parsnips, scrubbed and cut into matchsticks

2 endive heads, halved lengthwise

1 small eggplant, cut into thick wedges

2 sweet red or green bell peppers, seeded and halved lengthwise

1 small zucchini, halved lengthwise

2 fresh rosemary sprigs

2 fresh sage sprigs

1 teaspoon sea salt

½ teaspoon freshly ground black pepper

Position a rack in the center of the oven and preheat the oven to 400°F.

Pour ¼ cup of the oil in the bottom of a 13 × 9-inch baking pan and lay all of the vegetables flat. The pan will be full, but try to keep everything in one layer, tucking the vegetables close to each other so they remain succulent during the cooking process. This is key; otherwise they may dry out. Since the matchstick vegetables are thin, push them in a little pile or bunch; they tend to cook faster, and this keeps them from wilting. All will cook at different rates, and you will want to remove the vegetables as they finish roasting. For instance, the whole potatoes will take longer to cook than the eggplant or endive. Evenly pour the remaining ¼ cup oil over the vegetables. Tuck rosemary and sage sprigs into the vegetables, and season with the salt and pepper. Be liberal with both salt and pepper, as they will help to enhance the flavor of the vegetables.

Roast the vegetables for 20 minutes. Remove the pan from the oven and flip the vegetables so they cook evenly. Reduce the oven temperature to 325°F, return the pan to the oven, roast for another 20 minutes, and then check to see if the delicate vegetables are done. Remove the vegetables as they are ready, placing them on a warm serving dish, neatly and colorfully arranged. Tent the dish loosely with foil to keep warm. Return the pan to the oven for 10 minutes more, or until all the vegetables are done.

FENNEL AND WATERMELON SALAD SERVES 4

Nothing fancy, yet a nice change from a green salad to serve alongside a vegetable burger or grilled panini with cheese and roasted peppers. Try adding a few heirloom West Indian Burr gherkins sliced and tossed into the bowl.

1 medium fennel bulb, preferably Florence, halved, cored, and thinly sliced, fronds reserved for garnish

½ small watermelon, cut into 1-inch chunks (about 4 cups)

4 ripe red or yellow heirloom tomatoes, preferably Black Krim or Persimmon, cut into ½-inch wedges

1 head of loose-leaf lettuce, preferably Deer Tongue or Bibb

Yogurt Dressing (recipe at right)

½ cup crumbled feta cheese

In a large salad bowl, combine the fennel, watermelon, and tomatoes. Tear the lettuce into large pieces and add them to the bowl.

Spoon the dressing over the salad to taste; toss to coat. Crumble the feta cheese on top and gently toss. Garnish with the reserved fennel fronds and serve immediately.

YOGURT DRESSING
Makes about ½ cup

½ cup whole-milk yogurt

3 tablespoons extra-virgin olive oil

1 tablespoon balsamic vinegar

Zest and juice of 1 lemon

½ teaspoon sea salt

½ teaspoon freshly ground black pepper

In a small jar with a lid, combine the yogurt, oil, vinegar, lemon zest and juice, salt, and pepper. Shake vigorously to blend. Refrigerate leftovers for up to a week.

CARROT-ORANGE MARMALADE

MAKES 6 HALF-PINTS

The natural pectin in the lemon and orange peels means that no additional commercial pectin is required for this sunny marmalade. It takes longer to cook, yet the flavor is deepened. Invest in a candy thermometer for an accurate reading of the cooked jam.

2 medium organic lemons

2 medium organic oranges

8 medium organic carrots (1 pound), coarsely shredded (about 4 cups)

2½ cups sugar

Prepare 6 half-pint-size mason jars, lids, and rings (see page 174).

Slice the lemons and oranges in half crosswise and remove the seeds; keep the skins on all the fruit, which will create natural pectin. Chop the halves into smaller pieces and process in a food processor fitted with the steel blade until only fine bits remain.

In a heavy saucepan over medium heat, combine the lemons, oranges, carrots, sugar, and 4 cups water. Simmer until thick and syrupy, stirring occasionally, about 30 minutes. Test for doneness with a candy thermometer (it should reach 220°F); alternatively, drop ½ teaspoon onto a plate and put it in the freezer. It should thicken up quickly once cooled.

When the marmalade is ready, ladle it through a wide-mouth funnel into the prepared mason jars, leaving ¼ inch of headspace. Wipe the rims clean, place the lids on top, screw on the rings, and turn the jars upside down to start the sealing process. Meanwhile, prepare a hot-water bath. Lower the jars into the pot and boil for 10 minutes. Remove and cool the jars at room temperature, then label them. Store in a cool, dark cupboard.

THE GOURD FAMILY

Cucurbitaceae

EDIBLE SPECIES:
cucumber, gourd, melon, pumpkin, squash

One of the largest vegetable families for gardeners, this group includes cucumbers, melons, pumpkins, and summer and winter squashes, as well as gourds and chayotes. Most produce long vines with twining tendrils that climb vertically on a trellis before setting fruit, which tends to be globular in shape. All are prolific seed bearers, containing seeds inside rather than from an external flower, and pollination between species is frequent. If you plan to save seeds, isolate varieties for success.

CHILLED CUCUMBER SUMMER SOUP SERVES 4

The no-cook nature of this soup brings out the best in fresh cucumbers blended with fresh herbs.

6 lemon cucumbers, or 2 standard-size cucumbers, preferably Boston Pickling

2 cups plain whole-milk yogurt or kefir

1 medium fennel bulb, preferably Florence, coarsely chopped (about ¾ cup), fronds reserved

1 small red onion, preferably Red Torpedo, finely chopped (about ½ cup)

2 large eggs, hard-boiled and peeled

¼ cup chopped pecans, lightly toasted in a dry skillet

2 tablespoons chopped fresh dill

1 tablespoon chopped fresh mint

1 tablespoon chopped fresh Italian flat-leaf parsley

1 tablespoon extra-virgin olive oil

Salt and freshly ground black pepper

Trim the ends off the cucumbers and coarsely chop them—no need to remove seeds or peel. Place them in a blender along with the yogurt, chopped fennel, onion, eggs, pecans, dill, mint, parsley, and oil, and puree. The mixture will be thick. Taste and season with salt and pepper.

Transfer the soup to a bowl or a pitcher, cover, and refrigerate until chilled. Serve cold, garnished with the fennel fronds.

HEIRLOOM CULTIVARS IN THE GOURD FAMILY

CUCUMBER: *Lemon, Armenian, West Indian Gherkin, Boothby's Blonde, Poona Kheera, White Wonder*

MELON: *Jenny Lind, Charentais, Boule d'Or, Amish, Bidwell Casaba, Moon and Stars, Eden's Gem, Crenshaw, Green Nutmeg, Golden Honeymoon, Ha'ogen, Petit Gris de Rennes*

PUMPKIN: *Rouge Vif d'Etampes, Galeux d'Eysines, Musquee de Provence, Amish Pie, Winter Luxury Pie, Howden, Luminosa*

SUMMER SQUASH: *Costata Romanesco, Black Beauty, Zucchetta Rampicante (Tromboncino), Crookneck, Ronde de Nice, Lemon, Nimba, White or Yellow Scallop (Pattypan), Striata d'Italia*

WINTER SQUASH: *Marina di Chioggia, Butternut, Long Island Cheese, Kabocha, Red Kuri, Sibley, Blue Hubbard, Queensland Blue, Delicata*

PUMPKIN AND APPLE BISQUE

SERVES 4

French heirlooms Galeux d'Eysines or Rouge Vif d'Etampes will not only decorate your porch, they have exceptional flavor. Save the seeds, which can be dried and used in next year's garden.

1 small pumpkin
(about 2 pounds), preferably
Galeux d'Eysines or
Rouge Vif d'Etampes

1 yellow onion,
peeled and cut in half

2 large apples, preferably
Cortland, cored and quartered

1¼ cups full-fat coconut milk

1¼ cups boiling water

¼ cup apple cider vinegar

1 (1-inch) knob of fresh ginger,
peeled and diced
(2½ teaspoons)

1 teaspoon sea salt

1 teaspoon curry powder

½ teaspoon ground cinnamon

¼ teaspoon freshly ground
black pepper

Dash of grated nutmeg

Crème fraîche or yogurt,
for garnish

Preheat the oven to 425°F. Line a baking sheet with parchment paper.

Using a sharp knife, slice the pumpkin in half at the stem end. Scoop out the seeds and save to dry, if you like. Slice each half into thirds, creating six pieces, and place them, cut side down, on the prepared baking sheet. Place the onion halves on the baking sheet along with the apples. Bake until the pumpkin is tender and easily pierced with a fork, 35 to 40 minutes. Remove from the oven and let cool.

Use a spoon to carefully scoop out the pumpkin flesh, discarding the skin, and transfer the flesh to a blender along with the onion, apples, coconut milk, boiling water, vinegar, ginger, salt, curry powder, cinnamon, pepper, and nutmeg. Blend on high speed until silky smooth, about 2 minutes. Ladle the hot soup into bowls, garnish with crème fraîche, and serve.

CLASSIC BREAD-AND-BUTTER PICKLES MAKES 8 PINTS

Brining or immersing cucumbers in salty water extracts moisture, which keeps pickles crisp. Plan to use real pickling cucumbers, which are small with a dry interior and fewer seeds and can be quartered, while larger cucumbers are best sliced.

24 whole pickling cucumbers, preferably Boston Pickling, 4 to 6 inches long (about 8 pounds)

6 small yellow onions, thinly sliced (2½ cups)

1 cup pickling or kosher salt

6 cups apple cider vinegar

6 cups sugar

½ cup yellow mustard seeds

1 tablespoon celery seeds

2 hot peppers, preferably Long Red Cayenne, seeded and minced

8 fresh grape leaves (optional)

Slice the cucumbers lengthwise into quarters or into ¼-inch-thick rounds and place them in a large bowl. Add the onions and salt, and toss. Add enough cold water to cover the cucumbers, cover the bowl with a tea towel, and let them soak for at least 3 hours or overnight. Drain the cucumbers and onions in a large colander and rinse well under cold water.

In a large stainless-steel or enameled pot, bring the vinegar, sugar, mustard seeds, celery seeds, and hot peppers to a boil over high heat. Stir in the cucumbers and onions, and reduce the heat to low. Keep cooking for another 5 minutes, until the cucumbers soften slightly.

Wash and sterilize 8 pint-size mason jars (see page 174). If you're using grape leaves, add one to each sterilized jar. Ladle the hot cucumbers, onions, and brine through a wide-mouth funnel into the jars, distributing the brine and cucumbers equally and leaving ¼ inch of headspace.

Wipe the rims clean, place rubber lids on top, and screw on the rings tightly. Turn the jars upside down to start the sealing process. Prepare the hot-water bath and gently lower the jars into the boiling water on a rack. Boil for 10 minutes. Remove and cool the jars, and label with the contents and date. Store in a cool, dark place for at least 1 month before opening.

WINTER SQUASH PIE *with Rum*

SERVES 8

Blue Hubbard squash is a staple in most New England farm kitchens. Traditionally, it would be stored in a root cellar with pieces carved out, wedge by wedge, leaving the remaining squash in the cool room to last through the winter. A 2-pound wedge of Blue Hubbard squash, cooked as noted below, will yield about 2 cups of cooked puree for this recipe.

2 cups cooked and pureed winter squash, preferably Blue Hubbard (see Note)

½ cup granulated sugar

½ cup packed dark brown sugar

¼ cup dark rum

1 tablespoon unsulfured molasses

1½ teaspoons ground cinnamon

¼ teaspoon ground ginger

¼ teaspoon ground cloves

2 large eggs

1 cup heavy cream, heated just to scalding

Favorite Pastry Crust (recipe follows)

Whipped cream, for serving

Preheat the oven to 450°F.

In a blender, combine the pureed squash, both sugars, rum, molasses, cinnamon, ginger, and cloves, and whip until well blended, 3 to 5 minutes. Blend in the eggs one at a time, and then add the scalded cream. Keep the blender on for another few minutes to beat the eggs and give the mixture air.

Place the prepared piecrust on a baking sheet. Pour the filling into the crust. Bake 10 minutes; reduce the oven temperature to 325°F and continue baking until a knife inserted in the center comes out clean, about 40 minutes more. Transfer to a wire rack and cool completely. Serve at room temperature with whipped cream.

NOTE: To make the squash puree, preheat the oven to 375°F. Cut 2 pounds of the squash into 2-inch wedges or quarters, place them cut-side down in a roasting pan, and pour in ½ inch of water. Bake until the flesh is tender, about 1 hour. Cool; scoop out and discard the seeds. Mash the flesh with a fork to make a puree.

FAVORITE PASTRY CRUST

Makes one 10-inch crust

1½ cups unbleached
all-purpose flour or a mix
of all-purpose and
whole-wheat flours,
plus more for rolling

½ teaspoon sea salt

8 tablespoons (1 stick)
unsalted butter, chilled and
cut into ½-inch pieces

½ cup plain
whole-milk yogurt

The beauty of this crust recipe is that it does not need to be chilled in advance in order to roll out easily. The pastry dough comes together beautifully into a pliable ball, which is pressed gently to flatten and then rolled out effortlessly to the desired size. Transfer it to a pie pan and add the filling—voilà!

In the bowl of a food processor fitted with the metal blade, pulse together the flour and salt. With the machine whirring, add the butter, one piece at a time, until it is fully incorporated and the mixture looks like cornmeal. With the machine still whirring, add the yogurt, 1 tablespoon at a time, until the dough pulls together into a ball.

With your hands, scoop out the dough and press together all the tiny floury bits to form a pliable ball. Lightly flour the counter or a marble board and, with a rolling pin, roll out the dough, starting from the center and working your way to the edges. Roll into a 12-inch disk, about ⅛ inch thick, and slide the dough into a 10-inch pie pan, leaving a 1-inch overhang. Fold under and decoratively flute the edges. Refrigerate the crust until ready to fill.

BETTER HOMEMADE

Canning is fun and gives you the satisfaction of saying, "I made this!" Here's a short primer that will get you started.

HOW TO STERILIZE JARS AND LIDS

Always use heatproof jars, which are commonly known as mason jars. These are sold with lids that contain two parts: a top with a rubber seal that will adhere to the top of the glass jar when it is processed, and a screw-on ring. The lids with the rubber seal are used only once, to be replaced with fresh ones that can be purchased in bulk. The rings can be used many times over. Jars should be sterilized before filling, by either running them through a dishwasher or scrubbing them clean with soapy water and placing them upside down in a kettle of boiling water for 10 minutes; keep them inverted in the hot water (or in the dishwasher) until just before filling. Lids should *not* be boiled, or the rubber may not seal properly; instead, place them in a bowl and pour hot water over them to keep them warm.

HOW TO FILL THE JARS

Set the jars on the counter with a kitchen towel underneath to catch any drippings. Place a wide-mouth funnel inside the top of the jar and ladle the hot cooked filling (e.g., preserves, chutney) into the jar, leaving ¼ to ½ inch of headspace (as instructed in the recipe) at the top. Continue filling each of the jars, making sure they are evenly filled. Dip a paper towel into hot water and wipe the rim of each jar clean. It is important to make sure the rims are completely clean, which will prevent any mold from growing. Place the lid with the rubber seal on top of the jar rim, and gently screw on a ring top. Don't screw it too tightly, just enough to close and seal. Flip the jars upside down to start the sealing process; meanwhile, if necessary, bring a large kettle of water to a boil for the next step, called a hot-water bath. Most jams and jellies do not need to be processed in a hot-water bath; simply turn them over to seal the jar, flipping them right side up after 10 minutes.

FINAL STEP: THE HOT-WATER BATH

Fill a large stockpot with water, cover, and bring to a boil. Lower the filled and sealed hot jars onto a rack to keep the jars from touching the bottom. There should be enough water to cover the jars by 1 inch. Bring the water back to a boil and cook for the required amount of time, which is usually about 10 minutes. (Tomatoes and other low-acid fruits require specific canning instructions.) Carefully lift the rack with the jars from the hot-water bath and set the jars on the counter to cool. Wipe each cooled jar clean, label it with its contents and date, and store it in a cool, dark place for up to 2 years.

SUMMER SQUASH SOUP

with Parsley-Mint Pistou SERVES 6

Coconut milk is what gives this delicious summer soup an edge, along with a swirl of minty pistou. Native to Provence, pistou is similar to pesto, but without nuts or cheese—just the intense herbaceous flavor contained in a light sauce. Serve the soup chilled in a cup, or fill small mason jars to take along on a hike or picnic.

2 tablespoons butter

1 large onion, chopped

2 garlic cloves, finely chopped

1 tablespoon curry powder

1 teaspoon ground ginger

½ teaspoon ground turmeric

3 zucchini, preferably Costata Romanesco, coarsely chopped

4 small potatoes, preferably Carola or Desiree

½ cup unsweetened coconut milk, or to taste

Salt and pepper to taste

Parsley-Mint Pistou
(recipe at right)

Melt the butter in a large pot over medium heat. Add the onion and garlic and cook, stirring occasionally, until the onion is softened, about 5 minutes. Add the curry powder, ginger, and turmeric and stir until very fragrant, about 30 seconds.

Add the zucchini and potatoes and cover. Cook, stirring often, until they begin to soften, about 5 minutes. Add 6 cups water and bring to a boil. Reduce the heat to medium-low, cover, and simmer until the vegetables are tender, about 30 minutes.

With an immersion blender, puree the soup, adding just enough coconut milk to reach the desired consistency and flavor. Season lightly with salt and pepper. Cover and refrigerate until chilled. Swirl 1 tablespoon pistou into each bowl of cold soup just before serving.

PARSLEY-MINT PISTOU

Makes ½ cup

½ cup loosely packed fresh
Italian flat-leaf parsley leaves

¼ cup loosely packed
fresh mint leaves

1 shallot, chopped

¼ cup extra-virgin olive oil

½ teaspoon sea salt

Place the herbs and shallot in the bowl of a food processor and pulse until finely chopped. With the motor running, add the oil in a slow, steady stream. Add 2 tablespoons water and the salt, blending until smooth.

MEET THE GOURD FAMILY

CUCUMBER

Cucumbers grow on vigorous vines, often producing a bounty of smooth, crisp green fruit, eaten fresh or made into sweet pickles. Boston Pickling cucumber remains relatively unchanged since its early introduction in 1880, despite breeding efforts to develop new cucumber varieties. Best harvested when small and before seeds develop for a crisper pickle.

MELON

Several types of cantaloupe melons belong in the heirloom garden including Jenny Lind, a muskmelon that is named after the famous nineteenth-century singer who was known for her soprano voice. Charentais was introduced in France during the 1920s, and is a true cantaloupe type with a smooth creamy-gray exterior and sweet-tasting orange interior.

PUMPKIN

Pumpkins come in all shapes and sizes, yet surely one of the most gorgeous pumpkins of all is known as the Cinderella pumpkin because of its iconic shape. It can weigh between 15 and 20 pounds and resembles a cheese wheel when fully grown. A French heirloom originally offered by the Vilmorin seed company in the mid-1800s, this flat-topped variety turns a reddish-orange hue when left on the front porch through autumn.

WINTER SQUASH

Winter squash has been a mainstay of gardens, yet of all the varieties, Blue Hubbard has earned a place in history. Seeds came to North America in the 1800s with a sea captain returning home from explorations in South America; because it can reach a sizable 15 pounds per squash and stores beautifully all winter, it quickly became a favorite of American homestead gardeners.

THE SUNFLOWER FAMILY

Asteraceae or Compositae

EDIBLE SPECIES: *artichoke, calendula, cardoon, chicory and endive, echinacea, Jerusalem artichoke, lettuces, marigold, salsify, sunflower, tarragon*

Asteraceae or Compositae is one of the largest plant families, composed of both food and flowers. Most members are generally bitter tasting, even when cooked, and produce a distinctive daisy-like flower that forms a seed-producing pod. Many have long been regarded as containing properties that benefit the human body.

MEET THE SUNFLOWER FAMILY

ARTICHOKE

One of the most ornamental edibles for a kitchen garden, artichokes pair gray-green, tooth-shaped foliage with purple-tinged buds. Artichoke plants can be a little tricky to grow, depending on your location. Start seeds early in the spring, and set out seedlings when the weather is still cool—plants need a light frost to establish the budding cycle.

Sant'Erasmo is a little island north of Venice that is celebrated as having the best soil for growing vegetables—especially its famed namesake artichoke, which is protected as a cultural heritage plant in Italy and has become a local delicacy.

JERUSALEM ARTICHOKE

This ornamental daisy was once a major food source for Native Americans, before spreading throughout Europe. Despite its name, it has no relationship to Jerusalem or artichokes; Italians call them *girasole,* meaning "sunflower artichokes," because the taste of the roots is somewhat similar to that of an artichoke—yet certainly no substitute. The tops look like a wild daisy growing alongside the garden.

CHICORY

Chicory is a large family of plants popular in Italian cuisine, including Belgian endive, frisée, escarole, and radicchio, and many of the most celebrated heirloom varieties are named after the regions where they are a specialty. A wide range of leaf forms and variations of color can be found in most Italian markets, and seeds are easily grown in a kitchen garden. Chicories thrive in the Mediterranean climate, which makes them ideal for hot summers.

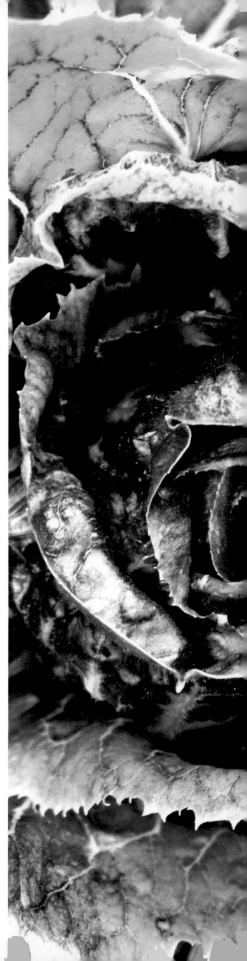

LETTUCE

For more than four thousand years, lettuce has been cultivated as a garden plant; its genus, *Lactuca,* derives its name from the Latin *lac* ("milk"), a reference to the milky sap that often comes from plants that have been allowed to go to seed. Hundreds of lettuces exist for the gardener, and lettuce continues to be one of the largest groups of garden plants grown from seed. Choose between butterhead, crisphead, loose-leaf, and romaine types.

Lettuce Forellenschluss is a romaine-type lettuce with green leaves splashed with burgundy red. Once prominent in European gardens, this unusual lettuce originated in Austria in 1793 and is also called Trout Back or Freckles. The flavor is light and buttery.

SALSIFY (AKA OYSTER ROOT)

Now a bit of a novelty, salsify is a nearly forgotten vegetable that was once a staple in most eighteenth-century gardens. The long taproot, the edible part, resembles a black stick and grows slightly larger than a narrow carrot or parsnip. Bring it into the kitchen, scrub clean, then boil or roast it until tender for a subtle oyster flavor, thus its nickname.

SPRING MESCLUN SALAD

with Lemon-Tahini Dressing   SERVES 4

Spring greens take well to a creamy dressing in which tahini gives a slightly nutty undertone to the lemony overtone.

6 cups mixed mesclun greens: lettuces, arugula, mâche, radicchio, young spinach, dandelion, purslane, curly endive, and/or sorrel

Lemon-Tahini Dressing (recipe follows)

½ cup chopped fresh spring herbs, such as mint, chives, and parsley, for garnish

Assorted edible flowers, such as wood viola, pansy, and/or chive blossoms, for garnish

To wash the mesclun greens, in a large bowl of cold water or in the sink, submerge the greens and gently stir them with your hands to shake any dirt (or bugs) loose. Let the greens sit for a few minutes, then gently lift them out and transfer to a colander.

Transfer the greens to a salad spinner to dry. Spread them in a single layer between paper towels, place them in a container, and chill in the refrigerator crisper drawer until ready to use. (This can be done the morning before preparing your salad.)

To prepare the salad, in a large bowl, gently toss the greens with ¼ cup of the dressing (about 1 tablespoon per serving). Taste the greens, adding more dressing or seasoning, if necessary. Divide evenly onto 4 chilled salad plates. Garnish with the herbs and flowers and serve.

LEMON-TAHINI DRESSING

Makes about ½ cup

¼ cup extra-virgin olive oil

¼ cup tahini

Juice of 1 lemon (about 3 tablespoons)

1 tablespoon honey

1 garlic clove, finely chopped

Sea salt and freshly ground black pepper

In a small jar with a lid, combine the oil, tahini, lemon juice, honey, and garlic. Shake vigorously or stir with a spoon to blend.

HEIRLOOM CULTIVARS IN THE SUNFLOWER FAMILY

ARTICHOKE: *Green Globe, Purple of Romagna, Violet de Provence*

CALENDULA: *Indian Prince, Flashback, Pacific Beauty, Resina*

CARDOON: *Rouge d'Alger, Gobbo di Nizzia*

CHICORY AND ENDIVE: *Variegata di Castelfranco radicchio, Catalogna Puntarelle, Chicoria Spadona, Rossa di Verona radicchio, Rossa di Treviso radicchio, Witloof Belgian endive*

JERUSALEM ARTICHOKE: *Mulles Rose, Jack's Copperclad, Waldboro Gold*

LETTUCE

    BUTTERHEAD: *Oak Leaf, Boston Buttercrunch, Black Seeded Simpson, Merveille de Quatre Saisons, Yugoslavian Red*

    CRISPHEAD: *Reine des Glaces, Pablo, Red Iceberg, Iceberg*

    LOOSE-LEAF: *Amish Deer Tongue, Grandpa Admire's, Lollo Rossa, Rossa di Trento*

    ROMAINE: *Little Gem, Rouge d'Hiver, Forellenschluss, Crisp Mint, Winter Density*

CARDOON GRATIN SERVES 4

There are not too many ways to serve cardoon, yet two classic Italian options exist: bagna cauda, which calls for dipping cardoon stems in hot anchovy-seasoned olive oil, and this creamy baked dish.

6 cardoon stalks,
preferably Tenderheart

3 cups heavy cream

1 cup vegetable stock,
preferably homemade

1 bay leaf

½ teaspoon sea salt

¼ teaspoon freshly ground
black pepper

2 tablespoons (¼ stick)
unsalted butter, softened,
for greasing

1 cup grated Gruyère cheese
(about ¼ pound)

1 cup toasted fresh
bread crumbs

6 fresh sage leaves, minced

Remove the tough outer stalks of the cardoon, cut away the thorns, and pull off the stringy fibers. If the stalks are extra large, slice each in half lengthwise and then crosswise into 4- to 6-inch pieces.

In a large saucepan, gently heat the cream, stock, bay leaf, salt, and pepper. Place the cardoon into the cream mixture, bring to a low simmer over low heat, and cook until tender, about 45 minutes.

Meanwhile, preheat the oven to 375°F. Use all of the butter to grease a 1-quart baking dish.

When the cardoon is tender, remove it with a slotted spoon and transfer it to the prepared baking dish, spreading it out evenly; set aside. Continue to simmer the cream mixture over medium heat until it is reduced to ¾ cup, about 10 minutes. Discard the bay leaf and pour the sauce over the cardoon. Sprinkle Gruyère, bread crumbs, and sage on top. Bake until bubbly, about 35 minutes. Serve hot.

STUFFED ARTICHOKES

with Herbed Bread Crumbs   SERVES 4

The leaves of artichokes are traditionally steamed and served with melted butter, but stuffing them with herbed bread crumbs transforms them into more of a meal.

4 large purple or green artichokes, preferably Purple of Romagna or Green Globe

½ cup fine dry bread crumbs

½ cup freshly grated Parmigiano-Reggiano cheese

2 garlic cloves, minced

2 tablespoons chopped fresh mint

2 tablespoons chopped fresh Italian flat-leaf parsley

1½ teaspoons coarse sea salt

¼ teaspoon freshly ground black pepper

½ cup extra-virgin olive oil

With a sharp knife, cut the bottom stem off each artichoke so that it will sit flat. Trim ½ inch from the top of each artichoke. With scissors, snip off the pointy tips from all the leaves.

In a food processor, combine the bread crumbs, cheese, garlic, mint, parsley, ½ teaspoon of the salt, and the pepper, and whir to finely chop the herbs and blend the ingredients. Add the oil in a slow stream.

Gently spread open each layer of artichoke leaves and fill each artichoke with about ¼ cup of the bread-crumb mixture, using a spoon or your fingers to press the mixture gently inside the artichoke and distribute it evenly.

Place the artichokes in a heavy saucepan that is just large enough to hold them all snugly so they won't tip over. Dust the tops with the remaining bread crumbs and press the leaves back together.

Add water to a depth of 1 inch and the remaining 1 teaspoon salt to the pan and bring it to a boil. Reduce the heat to low, cover the pot, and simmer for 30 minutes. Test for doneness by inserting a sharp knife through the center of an artichoke, or pull out a leaf and taste for tenderness.

Lift the cooked artichokes from the pot with tongs and serve them on individual plates (along with plenty of napkins).

FALL MESCLUN SALAD
with Garlic-Maple Vinaigrette SERVES 4

Spring mesclun is often milder than fall-grown greens, yet the dressing used here is slightly sweet, a little assertive, and simple to whisk together in a salad bowl or shake in a jar.

6 cups mixed mesclun greens: lettuces, arugula, mâche, radicchio, young spinach, purslane, curly endive, chervil, and/or cress

Garlic-Maple Vinaigrette (recipe follows)

Assorted edible flowers, such as wood viola, pansy, and/or chive blossoms, for garnish

Harvest the greens, either leaf by leaf or by the whole head. Wash and dry them thoroughly, and tear the leaves into bite-size pieces—do not cut with scissors or a knife!

Toss the greens lightly with the vinaigrette to taste, allowing about 2 tablespoons per serving. (Some people serve dressing on the side, but this usually results in a big glug rather than a refined, measured touch.) Garnish with the flowers and serve right away.

GARLIC-MAPLE VINAIGRETTE

Makes about ½ cup

1 teaspoon Dijon mustard

2 large garlic cloves, preferably German Red, pressed and finely chopped

1 teaspoon pure maple syrup

1 tablespoon fresh lemon juice

3 tablespoons balsamic vinegar

1 tablespoon finely chopped fresh sweet basil, preferably Genovese

½ cup extra-virgin olive oil

¼ teaspoon sea salt

⅛ teaspoon freshly ground black pepper

In a small jar with a lid, combine the mustard, garlic, maple syrup, lemon juice, vinegar, basil, oil, salt, and pepper. Shake vigorously to blend.

THE NIGHTSHADE FAMILY

Solanaceae

EDIBLE SPECIES:
*eggplant,
ground-cherry,
pepper, potato,
tomatillo, tomato*

After tasting tomatoes in France, Thomas Jefferson brought seeds to Monticello in the 1780s, planting a "dwarf tomata" and a large, ribbed "Spanish tomata." The curious plant, along with other members of the Solanaceae family, was not immediately popular, since some members of this family are poisonous. Fast-forward two hundred years, and these are the most popular crop in almost every home garden. On the flip side, there are tobacco, datura, mandrake, and belladonna, which produce aromatic night-scented flowers. Because this family continues to be one of the most enjoyed, it has also been the easiest to expand, with numerous heirlooms at its center.

EGGPLANT CAPONATA

MAKES ABOUT 4 CUPS; SERVES 8

A condiment made with eggplant and other summer vegetables, this recipe makes a large portion; any extra can be stored in a sealed container in the refrigerator for up to ten days.

½ cup extra-virgin olive oil, plus more for greasing

2 red onions, preferably Red Torpedo, cut into ½-inch dice

1 eggplant, preferably Black Beauty, peeled and cut into ¾-inch cubes

1 zucchini, preferably Costata Romanesco, cut into ¼-inch-thick rounds

1 large fennel bulb, preferably Florence, sliced

2 celery stalks, sliced

1 large red bell pepper, preferably Marconi Red, cut into ½-inch dice

3 garlic cloves, crushed

1 teaspoon sea salt

½ teaspoon freshly ground black pepper

½ cup balsamic vinegar

¼ cup coarsely chopped pitted oil-cured black olives

½ cup tomato paste

2 tablespoons capers

1 fresh oregano sprig, leaves finely chopped

Preheat the oven to 400°F. Lightly oil a large roasting pan and add the onions, eggplant, zucchini, fennel, celery, and bell pepper. Mix the ½ cup oil and the garlic in a measuring cup and drizzle it over the vegetables; sprinkle with the salt and pepper. Roast, stirring occasionally, until the vegetables are barely tender, about 30 minutes.

Whisk the vinegar, olives, tomato paste, capers, and oregano in a large bowl to dissolve the tomato paste. Pour this over the vegetables in the roasting pan and gently stir with a wooden spoon.

Continue to roast, stirring occasionally, until all the vegetables are soft and tender, about 30 minutes more.

Remove the pan from the oven and allow the vegetables to cool to room temperature in the pan. Taste and season generously with more salt and pepper. Stir before serving as a side dish or on toasted crusty bread as an appetizer.

HEIRLOOM TOMATO SALAD

SERVES 4

The range of colors in an heirloom tomato garden includes purple, green, red, orange, and yellow, which are especially beautiful when served on a large platter, thinly sliced and layered with mozzarella cheese and basil vinaigrette.

6 medium heirloom tomatoes,
preferably a mix of colors
(3 pounds)

¾ pound fresh mozzarella
cheese, thinly sliced

½ cup lemon basil
or sweet Genovese
basil leaves

2 garlic cloves,
finely chopped

¼ cup extra-virgin olive oil

Juice of 1 lemon

1 teaspoon sugar

Sea salt and
freshly ground
black pepper

Cut the tomatoes into ½-inch-thick slices and place them, over-lapping slightly, in a single layer in a shallow dish. Insert slices of mozzarella between the tomatoes.

If the basil leaves are small, layer whole leaves between the tomatoes. Alternatively, finely slice the basil into thin ribbons and scatter them on top. (The edges of cut basil may turn black, but this will be slightly tempered when you add the dressing in the next step.)

In a small bowl, whisk together the garlic, oil, lemon juice, and sugar. Season with salt and pepper. Pour the dressing evenly over the tomatoes, cover loosely, and let stand at room temperature to marinate for up to 30 minutes.

GOLDEN TOMATO GAZPACHO

SERVES 6

Made with yellow tomatoes and sweetened with a peach or an orange, this refreshing summer gazpacho has a hint of sweet citrus and stunning color.

1 medium peach
or navel orange, peeled and
cut into 1-inch pieces

4 medium yellow tomatoes,
preferably Persimmon,
coarsely chopped (2 cups)

2 sweet red, orange, or
yellow bell peppers, seeded
and coarsely chopped (2 cups)

1 medium cucumber,
peeled and coarsely chopped
(1½ cups)

½ sweet red onion,
finely chopped (½ cup)

1 garlic clove, minced

¼ cup fresh sweet Genovese
basil leaves, coarsely chopped,
plus more leaves for garnish

¾ cup extra-virgin olive oil

¼ cup sherry vinegar or red
wine vinegar

½ red cayenne hot pepper,
finely chopped (1 teaspoon)

½ teaspoon sea salt

½ teaspoon freshly ground
black pepper

Toasted bread croutons
and crème fraîche,
for garnish

Place the peach, tomatoes, peppers, cucumber, onion, and garlic in a blender or food processor fitted with the steel blade. Pulse to coarsely chop. Add the chopped basil, oil, vinegar, hot pepper, salt, and black pepper. Pulse to blend, either until smooth or keeping a few chunks for texture. Cover and refrigerate until well chilled, at least 1 hour.

Taste the soup and season with more salt and pepper if necessary. Serve in chilled bowls, garnishing each with croutons, a swirl of crème fraîche, and basil leaves.

HEIRLOOM CULTIVARS IN THE NIGHTSHADE FAMILY

EGGPLANT: *Prosperosa, Cookstown Orange, Casper White, Korean Red, Lao Purple Stripe, Listada de Gandia, Melanzane Rosso di Beauty, Little Fingers*

PEPPER

SPICY: *Black Hungarian, Anaheim, ghost (Bhut Jolokia), Brazilian Starfish, Long Red Cayenne, habanero, McMahon's Texas Bird, Thai Hot*

SWEET: *Chocolate Beauty, Corno di Toro, Friariello di Napoli, Golden Marconi, Jimmy Nardello, Lilac Bell, Apple, Alma Paprika, Purple Beauty, Orange Bell, Buran*

POTATO: *Russet Burbank, Yukon Gold, Rose Finn Apple, Purple Viking, German Butterball, French Fingerling, Carola, Purple Peruviane*

TOMATO: *Brandywine, Big Rainbow, Purple Calabash, Cherokee Purple, Anna Russian, Green Zebra, Speckled Roman, Mortgage Lifter—and hundreds more!*

FRESH MAPLE-TOMATO SALSA

MAKES 8 CUPS

Say good-bye to commercial salsa forevermore. A snack or appetizer with chips, this spicy and sweet condiment brings together the bright, lively flavors of fresh tomatoes, peppers, and onions.

6 medium ripe heirloom
tomatoes (3 pounds),
preferably Brandywine
or Purple Calabash

2 medium onions,
finely diced

2 sweet red or green peppers,
preferably Corno di Toro,
seeded and diced

1 habanero chile pepper,
seeded and diced

1 jalapeño pepper,
seeded and diced

2 garlic cloves, minced

¼ cup chopped fresh dill

¼ cup chopped fresh Italian
flat-leaf parsley

¼ cup chopped fresh cilantro

1 lemon, juiced

1 lime, juiced

1 teaspoon coarse sea salt

1 teaspoon ground cumin

⅓ cup pure maple syrup

2 tablespoons soy sauce

Trim the tops off the tomatoes and gently squeeze out the juice and the seeds from the interior cavities. Coarsely chop the tomato into ½-inch pieces; there should be about 5 cups chopped tomatoes. Place in a large mixing bowl.

Add the onions to the tomatoes, along with the diced peppers, habanero, jalapeño, and garlic, and stir to combine.

Add the dill, parsley, cilantro, lemon and lime juices, salt, cumin, maple syrup, and soy sauce. Stir to blend. Serve immediately while fresh, or allow to sit in the refrigerator overnight for the flavors to meld. Fresh salsa will keep for a week in the refrigerator.

HUSK GROUND-CHERRY CLAFOUTI SERVES 8

The first time you taste a husk ground-cherry, your taste buds will buzz with pineapple, butterscotch, and mango flavors. These sweet cousins of tomatoes can be eaten fresh off the vine or baked into a rich, custardy clafouti.

2 tablespoons (¼ stick) unsalted butter, at room temperature, for greasing

2 cups ripe husk ground-cherries, preferably Aunt Molly's, or pitted cherries or berries of choice

¾ cup unbleached all-purpose flour

6 tablespoons granulated sugar

½ teaspoon sea salt

1¼ cups whole milk

2 tablespoons kirsch

1 tablespoon vanilla extract

6 eggs

2 tablespoons confectioners' sugar, for dusting

Position a rack in the center of the oven. Preheat the oven to 425°F.

Butter an 8½ × 12-inch baking dish or a medium cast-iron skillet. Remove the paper husks from the ground-cherries.

In a blender, combine the flour, granulated sugar, and salt. Slowly pour in the milk, kirsch, vanilla, and finally the eggs, one at a time, blending until smooth, 2 or 3 minutes.

Pour the batter into the prepared dish and evenly distribute the ground-cherries over the top. Bake for 30 minutes or until a skewer inserted into the center comes out clean and a golden crust has formed. Cool slightly. Serve the clafouti directly out of the baking dish, or run a butter knife around the edges and carefully flip it onto a serving platter or cutting board. Dust with confectioners' sugar right before serving.

POTATO SALAD
with Green Goddess Dressing   SERVES 4

Spoon lemony Green Goddess dressing over hot potatoes for an interesting take on potato salad.

2 pounds (about 8)
medium new red potatoes,
preferably Banana Fingerling

½ red onion,
finely chopped

½ cup Green Goddess
Dressing (recipe follows)

1 head of butterhead lettuce,
preferably Trout Back or
Tennis Ball

½ cup finely chopped
fresh chives

Bring a pot of lightly salted water to a boil. Place the unpeeled potatoes in a vegetable steamer basket and lower it into the boiling water. Cook the potatoes until tender when pierced with a sharp knife, about 30 minutes, depending on the size. Remove the steamer basket and potatoes and, when they are cool enough to handle, slice or quarter them.

Place the potatoes in a salad bowl with the red onions and spoon ¼ cup dressing on top. Toss to fully coat, adding more dressing as necessary, and refrigerate until chilled. Serve on a bed of soft butterhead lettuce leaves and garnish with the chives.

GREEN GODDESS DRESSING

Makes 1 cup

½ cup mayonnaise

½ cup sour cream

2 canned anchovy fillets

½ garlic clove, chopped

Juice of 1 lemon

¼ cup fresh basil leaves,
chopped

1 tablespoon fresh tarragon
leaves, chopped

1 tablespoon fresh parsley
leaves, chopped

Salt and freshly ground
black pepper

In a blender or food processor, combine the mayonnaise, sour cream, anchovies, garlic, lemon juice, and herbs. Blend until smooth, about 1 minute. Season with salt and pepper. Refrigerate in a mason jar for up to a week.

THE LEGUME FAMILY

Leguminosae or Fabaceae

EDIBLE SPECIES:
beans, chickpeas, favas, lentils, peanuts, peas, soybeans

Among the oldest cultivated plant families, legumes have sustained people all over the world for hundreds of centuries. Comprised primarily of beans, peas, peanuts, soybeans, chickpeas, tamarind, and lentils, this large group of edible plants deserves more appreciation and praise, especially the heirloom varieties.

The edible part of most legumes is grown inside seedpods that burst open when ripe and, if not harvested in time as a food crop, will disperse seeds. This was most likely how the first gardeners discovered that seeds could be planted and grown as a cultivated food crop, noticing these plants and subsequent generations growing nearby. Legumes have more capacity for longevity than any other seeds, and are best suited for long-term preservation by seed savers.

MEET THE LEGUME FAMILY

SHELLING BEAN Shelling beans are formed inside a pod, left to dry on the vine, and harvested at the end of the season. They have been widely grown for centuries, and nowadays most gardeners prefer to buy them than grow them. If you choose to do otherwise, consider the Christmas Lima, a distinctive chestnut-brown and white spotted bean, also called chestnut bean. Prized for its large and creamy texture similar to that of a buttery potato, it's especially good in soups and stews.

POLE BEAN Pole beans are grown vertically on poles or a trellis, and the beans can either be an edible pod bean or a shelling bean. They are ornamental and take up less space in a kitchen garden than a bush bean. When harvesting edible pod beans, it's important to harvest them when the beans are young and tender; left to grow larger than a pencil, they will become tough and stringy.

EDIBLE POD PEA There are two different types of edible pod peas: sugar snaps or flat podded, also known as a snow pea. Carouby de Maussane is a French variety with purple-blue flowers that give way to delectable sweet pods on vines that grow as much as five feet tall. Since it is getting harder to find them in the seed catalogs, save a few pods to grow into mature seeds for a second growing season.

SHUCKING PEA Shucking peas are grown for their tiny sweet orbs; the exterior pods are inedible. Considered a delicacy, the first shucking pea appeared in the court of Louis XIV and quickly became associated with high style. The vining plants can grow quite tall and require good staking.

BORLOTTO BEAN AND FARRO SALAD   SERVES 4

Borlotto beans, also known as cranberry beans, form a solid protein-rich base along with farro, for this colorful Italian vegetable salad.

1 cup fresh shelling beans, preferably Borlotto, soaked in water overnight

½ cup uncooked farro

¼ cup extra-virgin olive oil

Juice of 1 lemon

2 tablespoons balsamic vinegar

½ teaspoon sea salt

1 pint cherry tomatoes, halved

1 medium fennel bulb, preferably Florence, cut into slivers (about ¾ cup)

1 small red onion, preferably Red Torpedo, thinly sliced into half-moons

½ cup fresh sweet basil leaves, torn into bite-size pieces

1 cup radicchio leaves, torn into bite-size pieces

2 heads of endive, preferably Witloof Belgian, diced

½ cup shaved Parmigiano-Reggiano cheese

Drain and place the beans in a saucepan with water to cover. Over medium-low heat, bring to a simmer and cook uncovered for an hour or more, adding more water as necessary. (Freshly harvested beans will take less time than beans that have been completely dried; adjust the timing as needed.) When beans are soft and tender but before they break apart, turn off the heat. Drain.

In a 1-quart saucepan over medium heat, lightly brown the farro to give it a nutty flavor. Add 1½ cups water, bring to a boil, reduce the heat to a simmer, and cook, uncovered, until the water is absorbed, about 30 minutes. Drain and cool.

In a medium salad bowl, whisk together the oil, lemon juice, vinegar, and salt. Add the beans, farro, tomatoes, fennel, and onions. Let the vegetables marinate and soak up the dressing for 30 minutes.

Just before serving, toss the salad with the basil, radicchio, and endive, and top with the shaved cheese.

BAKED BEANS
with Maple and Molasses   SERVES 8

These are more like your grandmother's baked beans—made from real beans and not those dropped out of a can, bacon instead of pork fat, molasses instead of sugar.

1 pound fresh or dried heirloom shelling beans, preferably cranberry or Hidatsa Shield

1 tablespoon plus ½ teaspoon kosher salt

2 garlic cloves, minced (1 teaspoon)

2 medium yellow onions, peeled and coarsely chopped (2 cups)

2 bay leaves

6 slices thick-cut bacon (about ½ pound) or pork fat

1 cup packed dark brown sugar

1 cup dark unsulphured molasses

½ cup apple cider vinegar

¼ cup Dijon mustard

Freshly ground black pepper

Place the beans in a 6-quart stockpot and cover with boiling water by 2 inches. Add 1 tablespoon of the salt, stir, and soak for 2 hours or overnight, depending on whether the beans are fresh or dried.

Drain the beans in a colander and return them to the stockpot. Add water to cover by 2 inches and the remaining ½ teaspoon salt. Add ½ teaspoon of the garlic, 1 cup of the onion, and the bay leaves. Simmer over low heat, covered, until the beans are tender but not falling apart and most of the water has been absorbed, up to 1 hour. Remove from the heat. Place a colander over a medium bowl and drain the beans, reserving the liquid in the bowl. Remove the bay leaves.

Position a rack in the center of the oven and preheat the oven to 325°F.

With a sharp knife, chop the bacon into bite-size pieces and place it in a cast-iron Dutch oven or large, heavy cooking pot. Gently cook over medium-low heat until most of the fat is rendered yet the bacon is not crisp, about 15 minutes. Add the remaining 1 cup chopped onion and ½ teaspoon garlic and sauté until soft, about 5 minutes. Add the brown sugar, molasses, vinegar, and mustard. Stir in the cooked beans, a good grinding of black pepper, and just enough of the reserved bean liquid (up to 1 cup) to make a slightly soupy mixture.

Cover and bake until the beans are thick and look dark and glazed, about 1 hour. Check at the 45-minute mark to see if they need more liquid; stir in ½ cup of the bean liquid or water, if necessary. Taste and adjust seasonings. If the beans aren't completely soft, return them to the oven and bake up to another 30 minutes, until soft. When they're ready, remove from the oven and keep covered until ready to serve.

HEIRLOOM CULTIVARS IN THE LEGUME FAMILY

BEANS

FAVA: *Broad Windsor, Aquadulce, Martock, horse, or English*

SNAP: *Fin de Bagnol, Beurre de Rocquencourt, Blauhilde, Dragon's Tongue bush, Yellow or Green Anellino, Trionfo Violetto*

SHELLING: *Rattlesnake, Christmas Lima, Borlotto, scarlet runner, Lazy Wife, Kentucky Blue Wonder, Cherokee Trail of Tears, Hidatsa Red Indian Shield, Mayflower, Hutterite, Arikara Yellow, Turkey Craw, red cranberry*

PEAS

EDIBLE POD: *Carouby de Maussane, Mammoth Melting, Oregon Giant, Amish Snap, Dwarf Gray Sugar, Sugar Ann*

SHUCKING: *Green Arrow, Tom Thumb, Lincoln, Corne de Belier, Blue Podded Blauwschokkers, Waverex (petits pois), Sutton's Harbinger*

THE ROSE FAMILY

Rosaceae

EDIBLE SPECIES:
*almond, apple, apricot,
blackberry, peach,
pear, plum, quince,
raspberry, rose,
strawberry*

This family of flowering plants is responsible for some of our most prized culinary fruits and herbs, as well as ornamental shrubs and trees. Botanically, it takes a true scientist to follow the taxonomy that might explain the two hundred or so species, yet like most plant families, members can be primarily identified by their similarities, including the shape of the flowers, which have five solitary open petals surrounding a stamen, all fused together in a cuplike structure.

The stems on these primarily small shrubs, or sometimes trees, are generally woody and thorny, often growing as ramblers that can quickly become a little untamed. Not everyone has room to grow fruit trees or brambly berry vines, yet there are many ways to integrate at least one member of the rose family into the kitchen garden or landscape, because each species has a unique story of origin.

ARUGULA, CARAMELIZED PEAR, AND TOASTED WALNUT SALAD

SERVES 4

Cool late-autumn weather is ideal for arugula, which coincides nicely with pears and fresh cranberries. Put them together in this composed salad, dressed with a maple-sweetened vinaigrette, for a dish that is also art on a plate.

4 medium heirloom pears, preferably Bosc, cored and sliced lengthwise

½ cup fresh cranberries

2 tablespoons sugar

1 tablespoon unsalted butter, melted

½ cup shelled walnuts

3 tablespoons extra-virgin olive oil

1 tablespoon balsamic vinegar

1 garlic clove, finely minced

Salt and freshly ground black pepper

½ teaspoon Dijon mustard

½ teaspoon maple syrup

6 cups arugula or mixed salad greens

¼ cup freshly grated Parmigiano-Reggiano cheese

Place a rack in the center of the oven and preheat the oven to 400°F.

In a medium bowl, toss the pears and cranberries with the sugar and butter. Arrange the pears and cranberries in a single layer on a baking sheet. Bake, turning once, until the pears are barely tender, 10 to 15 minutes.

Lightly toast the walnuts in a dry skillet over medium heat until golden brown, 3 to 5 minutes. Remove from the heat and set aside.

In a large salad bowl, prepare the dressing by whisking together the oil, vinegar, garlic, salt and pepper to taste, mustard, and maple syrup. Add the arugula and toss to coat.

Divide the arugula among 4 chilled plates. Arrange one-fourth of the pears in a fan around the center of each plate and evenly sprinkle the cranberries, Parmigiano-Reggiano, and toasted nuts on top.

HEIRLOOM CULTIVARS IN THE ROSE FAMILY

APPLE: *Baldwin, Belle de Boskoop, Blue Pearmain, Bramley, Cortland, Cox's Orange Pippin, Esopus Spitzenburg, Golden Russet, Gravenstein, Lady, Lamb Abbey Pearmain, Macintosh*

PEAR: *Bartlett, Seckle, D'Anjou, Bartlett, Bosc, Blake's Pride, Potomac, Warren, Kieffer*

RASPBERRY: *Heritage, Latham, primocane, Royalty, Jewel Black, Taylor*

STRAWBERRY

ALPINE: *Regina, Scarlet, White Soul, Yellow Wonder, Fragola di Bosco, Attila, Baron von Solemacher*

EVERBEARING: *Fort Laramie, Quinault, Alexandria, Old North Sea, Tresca*

PEACH GINGER CHUTNEY MAKES 6 PINTS

Sweetened with ripe peaches, this chutney was adapted from a recipe handed down from a neighbor, who cautioned that making it is like driving on an icy road—"Take your time and don't be in a hurry."

2 cups packed dark brown sugar

2 cups apple cider vinegar

2 red onions, preferably Wethersfield Red, halved lengthwise and thinly sliced into half-moons (about 1 cup)

1 fresh red hot pepper, preferably Long Red Cayenne, seeded and minced

1 fresh jalapeño pepper, seeded and minced

1 tablespoon pickling or kosher salt

1 tablespoon yellow mustard seeds

4 pounds almost-ripe heirloom peaches, preferably Belle of Georgia (about 8 peaches)

1 cup dried cranberries or currants

¼ cup peeled and grated fresh ginger

In a large stockpot, over medium-high heat, bring the brown sugar and vinegar to a boil, stirring to dissolve the sugar. Stir in the onions, hot pepper, jalapeño, salt, and mustard seeds. Reduce the heat to medium and cook at a brisk simmer for 10 minutes.

Meanwhile, bring a large stockpot of water to a boil and then gently immerse the peaches. Remove them after 1 minute, drain, cool slightly in a colander, and slip off and discard the skins. Over a large bowl, pit the peaches and cut them into roughly ½- to 1-inch chunks; there should be about 6 cups. Drain the excess juice that collects in the bottom of the bowl (it is a delicious sweet nectar to drink!) and add the peaches to the simmering vinegar brine. Stir in the cranberries and ginger.

Continue to simmer over medium-low heat, stirring occasionally, until the peaches and the brine take on a glossy look, about 45 minutes. Take care not to overcook the peaches; they will cook again when the canning jars are processed, and it is nice to have a chunky chutney.

Wash and sterilize 6 pint-size mason jars (see page 174). Once the chutney is ready, fill the jars with the chutney; wipe the rims clean with a hot damp towel and screw on the sterilized lids. Flip the jars upside down to seal. Prepare the hot-water bath and gently lower the jars into the boiling water on a rack. Boil for 10 minutes, then remove and cool. Label the jars and set them on a shelf in a cool, dark place for a minimum of 3 months to allow the flavors to meld and ripen. (See page 174 for complete canning instructions.)

MÂCHE SALAD *with Pomegranate, Oranges, Plums, and Candied Pecans* SERVES 4

A European heirloom salad green that oddly is not seen much in this country, mâche—also known as feldsalat or corn salad—is a mild-tasting spoon-shaped green that grows in a delicate small rosette. It is best grown in the cool spring or late fall. Add any seasonal fruit, fresh or lightly grilled. such as heirloom Shiro plums.

CANDIED PECANS

½ cup pecan halves

1 tablespoon maple syrup

SALAD

⅓ cup pomegranate juice

⅓ cup extra-virgin olive oil

¼ cup red wine vinegar

1 tablespoon maple syrup

1 teaspoon Dijon mustard

½ teaspoon sea salt

¼ teaspoon freshly ground black pepper

8 cups mâche, preferably Vit, washed and dried

½ cup crumbled chèvre

1 shallot, finely chopped

4 tablespoons pomegranate seeds

1 blood orange or navel orange, peeled and cut into sections or bite-size pieces

2 or 3 plums, preferably Shiro, cut into wedges

In a small skillet over medium heat, cook the pecans and maple syrup until lightly toasted, about 5 minutes, stirring frequently to prevent burning. Set aside to cool.

In a small jar with a lid, combine the pomegranate juice, oil, vinegar, maple syrup, mustard, salt, and pepper. Shake vigorously to blend. Measuring out 2 tablespoons per serving, spoon the dressing over the mâche, and toss to coat. Taste and add more dressing, if desired.

Evenly divide the greens among 4 salad plates. Top each serving with an equal amount of chèvre, shallots, pomegranate seeds, orange pieces, plum wedges, and candied pecans. Serve right away.

ROSE HIP MARMALADE MAKES 6 PINTS

Rose hips turn into a thick, sumptuous jam with a gorgeous deep-red color. With a hint of citrus and crab apples, the end result is a complex and fruity spread.

6 cups bright-red wild rose hips, picked at their peak of ripeness

1 whole orange

1 whole lemon

6 crab apples, preferably Dolgo

5 cups sugar

½ teaspoon unsalted butter

To prepare the rose hips, trim the stem ends and discard them; cut the fruit in half. Scrape out the seeds and discard them. Roughly chop the rose hips; there should be about 4 cups.

Slice the orange, lemon, and apples lengthwise into wedges. Remove any seeds and cut each wedge in half crosswise to make bite-size triangles. Keep the peels intact, as they provide pectin.

In a deep 8-quart stockpot, combine the rose hips, orange, lemon, and apples. Add 6 cups water and bring the mixture to a boil. Reduce the heat to keep the jam at a low boiling point, stirring often, for about 30 minutes, or until the rose hips become soft.

Turn off the heat. Stir the sugar into the stockpot to combine. Turn the heat to high and keep stirring until the sugar is dissolved. Add the butter (which decreases the foam), reduce the heat to medium-high, and continue to cook until the jam reaches 220°F on a jelly thermometer; this may take about 15 minutes. Do not overcook, as that will give the marmalade an odd taste.

Divide and ladle the jam through a funnel into 6 hot sterilized pint-size canning jars (which can be sterilized in a hot-water bath or dishwasher; see page 174), leaving ¼ inch of headspace. Wipe the rims with a wet cloth to clean, place the lids on the jars, and seal them with a rim. Turn the filled jars upside down for 15 minutes to fully seal them, then flip right side up. Store in a cool pantry for up to 2 years.

SUMMER COBBLER SERVES 6

A buttermilk biscuit topping is seasoned with a touch of cardamom to complement the aromatic fruit. Top with vanilla ice cream for a summer treat.

FILLING

½ cup sugar

1 tablespoon cornstarch

⅛ teaspoon cinnamon

⅛ teaspoon sea salt

2 pints blueberries, preferably Blueray

1 pint raspberries, preferably Heritage Red

6 ripe peaches, preferably Red Haven, peeled and sliced

Zest and juice of 1 lemon

BISCUIT TOPPING

1 cup unbleached all-purpose flour

¼ cup plus 2 teaspoons sugar

2 tablespoons cornmeal

2 teaspoons baking powder

¼ teaspoon baking soda

¼ teaspoon salt

½ cup buttermilk

4 tablespoons (½ stick) unsalted butter, melted and cooled

½ teaspoon vanilla extract

½ teaspoon ground cardamom

⅛ teaspoon cinnamon

Position a rack in the center of the oven and preheat the oven to 375°F.

Make the filling: In a large bowl, stir together the sugar, cornstarch, cinnamon, and salt. Add the berries and the peaches, and mix gently until the fruit is evenly coated. Stir in the lemon zest and juice and transfer the mixture to a 9-inch glass pie pan. Place the pie pan on a baking sheet and bake for 25 minutes, or until hot and bubbly.

Make the biscuit topping: In a large bowl, whisk together the flour, ¼ cup of the sugar, the cornmeal, baking powder, baking soda, and salt. In a small bowl, whisk together the buttermilk, butter, and vanilla. In another small bowl, stir together the remaining 2 teaspoons sugar, the cardamom, and cinnamon to blend, and set aside until the berries come out of the oven.

A few minutes before the fruit emerges from the oven, finish the biscuits by adding the wet ingredients to the dry ingredients and stirring gently until just combined and no dry pockets remain.

Remove the hot bubbling fruit from the oven and raise the oven temperature to 425°F. Spoon 8 equal portions of biscuit dough evenly on the hot filling, spacing them at least ½ inch apart, and sprinkle each biscuit with a little reserved cinnamon-cardamom sugar. Bake until the filling is bubbling and the biscuits are golden brown and cooked through, about 15 minutes. Cool slightly before serving.

MIXED-BERRY MUFFINS MAKES 12 MUFFINS

Cakelike muffins at the peak of berry season—what could be better? Frozen berries work just as well in this recipe; defrost at room temperature and drain excess juice before adding to the batter.

2 tablespoons unsalted butter, at room temperature

2 cups unbleached all-purpose flour

1 tablespoon baking powder

½ teaspoon sea salt

½ teaspoon ground cinnamon

1 cup granulated sugar

½ cup vegetable oil

4 large eggs, at room temperature

1 teaspoon vanilla extract

1 teaspoon almond extract

1 cup plain yogurt

2 cups mixed berries (blueberries, raspberries, and blackberries)

¼ cup raw sugar, for topping

Position a rack in the center of the oven and preheat the oven to 375°F. Lightly brush the wells of a 12-cup muffin pan with the butter to coat (or insert paper muffin cups).

In a large bowl, mix the flour, baking powder, salt, and cinnamon. Beat the granulated sugar and oil in the bowl of a stand mixer on high speed until light and fluffy, about 2 minutes. Beat in the eggs, one at a time, then add the vanilla and almond extracts and the yogurt. Fold in the berries and spoon the batter evenly into the muffin cups, filling each one three-quarters full. Evenly sprinkle the tops with the raw sugar.

Bake until the muffins are golden brown and a toothpick inserted in the center comes out clean, about 40 minutes. Cool in the pan on a wire rack for 5 minutes before carefully removing the muffins from the pan.

THE KNOTWEED FAMILY

Polygonaceae

EDIBLE SPECIES:
*buckwheat,
rhubarb, sorrel*

Most gardeners could do without this family of plants—considered a pernicious weed—in the form of Japanese knotweed (Fallopia japonica). Yet if you love the taste of sorrel and rhubarb, the first harbingers of spring, you will learn to take pleasure in growing these in your heirloom kitchen garden.

The family name (Polygonaceae) is derived from the Latin roots poly ("many") and gona ("joints"). If you look at the plant form, bracts appear where new branches grow. Most of the plants in this family are hardy perennials, meaning that they will come back year after year for an abundance of food crops with little effort.

RHUBARB PIE *with Ginger and Lemon*

A good slice of pie to start the day in the garden begins here. A light crumb topping and subtle bite of ginger will bring you back into the kitchen for a second slice.

SINGLE PIECRUST

1¼ cups unbleached all-purpose flour, plus more for rolling

½ teaspoon sea salt

½ teaspoon sugar

½ cup (1 stick) unsalted butter, chilled and cut into ¼-inch chunks

FILLING

8 medium rhubarb stalks, leaves removed and discarded

1 cup whole cranberries, fresh or frozen

¼ cup dark rum

2 tablespoons peeled and grated fresh ginger

Zest and juice of 1 lemon

½ cup unbleached all-purpose flour

⅓ cup sugar

1 teaspoon ground cinnamon

Make the piecrust: In a cup or a small bowl, combine ½ cup water with several ice cubes and let sit for 5 minutes to completely chill until icy cold. Meanwhile, combine the flour, salt, and sugar in the bowl of a food processor and whir to combine. While pulsing the processor, add the butter to the flour piece by piece until all has been added and is well blended.

With the machine running, slowly pour in 3 tablespoons of the ice water and whir until the dough begins to form a ball. Stop the food processor and remove the dough with your hands, shaping it into a disk. Press it together to gather all the bits and slightly flatten it before wrapping it in wax paper. Refrigerate for an hour or so to chill into a cohesive disk.

When ready to roll out the dough, remove it from the refrigerator, unwrap it, and allow it to sit on a lightly floured surface for about 5 minutes. With a rolling pin and starting from the center, roll the dough out in every direction to make an even 12-inch circle; it should measure an inch or two larger than the pie dish. Fold the dough in half and gently transfer it to a pie dish. Fold and crimp the edges.

Position a rack in the bottom third of the oven and preheat the oven to 375°F.

Chop the rhubarb into 1-inch chunks; you should have about 6 cups. Place it in a large bowl along with the cranberries, dark rum, ginger, lemon zest and juice, and toss to blend. Add the flour, sugar, and cinnamon and gently stir to completely blend.

TOPPING

¼ cup (½ stick)
unsalted butter,
at room temperature

½ cup unbleached
all-purpose flour

¼ cup sugar

¼ cup pure maple syrup

Vanilla ice cream or fresh
ginger–infused whipped
cream, for serving

Prepare the topping: In a small bowl, combine the butter, flour, sugar, and maple syrup. With a fork, blend the ingredients together thoroughly; it will be a crumbly mixture.

To make the pie, pour the rhubarb filling into the crust and sprinkle evenly with the crumbly topping. Set the pie dish on a baking sheet and bake about 45 minutes, or until the topping is golden and the rhubarb is bubbling. Remove from the oven and cool to room temperature before serving with ice cream.

HEIRLOOM CULTIVARS IN THE KNOTWEED FAMILY

RHUBARB: *Victoria, Glaskins Perpetual*

SORREL: *Green de Belleville*

BUCKWHEAT CREPES

with Spicy Applesauce   MAKES 24 CREPES

Growing your own grains may be a thing of the past, but buckwheat is a good place to start. It's a bit of a chore to grind the kernels into flour, though; luckily, buckwheat flour is easily found in most markets. The nutty flavor is a wonderful complement to softened fall fruit.

½ cup whole-wheat flour

½ cup buckwheat flour

½ cup unbleached
all-purpose flour

1 teaspoon salt

4 large eggs

1 cup whole milk

4 tablespoons (½ stick)
unsalted butter, melted

Vegetable oil,
for the crepe pan

Spicy Applesauce
(recipe follows)

In a large mixing bowl, combine all the flours and salt. Add the eggs and mix with a whisk to blend. Gradually pour in the milk and 1¼ cups water, whisking vigorously to prevent lumps. Add the butter and continue to whisk until smooth.

Lightly oil an 8-inch crepe pan or shallow skillet and set it over medium heat. When the pan is warm, lift it from the heat, wait 3 seconds, and then pour in ¼ cup of the crepe batter while tilting the pan so the batter evenly coats the bottom. Return to the heat. Cook until lightly browned underneath, about 2 minutes. Flip the crepe with a thin spatula and cook the other side until lightly browned, about 1 minute more. Transfer to a plate, cover with another plate or a tea towel to keep it warm, and continue until all the crepes are made.

You can either fill the crepes while warm, let them cool completely, or store them in the refrigerator for up to 5 days. Reheat them in a dry skillet over medium-low heat for a nice crisp exterior.

To finish, spread about 3 tablespoons applesauce on each crepe. Fold the crepe in half or roll it into a tube, slice it in half, and serve.

SPICY APPLESAUCE

Makes 4 cups

½ cup sugar

Juice of ½ lemon
(about 1 tablespoon)

½ teaspoon ground cinnamon

¼ teaspoon freshly
grated nutmeg

¼ teaspoon ground ginger

⅛ teaspoon ground cloves

8 medium cooking apples
(2 pounds), preferably
Cortland or Macintosh,
unpeeled, cored, and
thinly sliced

The type of apple will determine the cooking time: a firm Cortland, for example, will take slightly longer to cook than a soft Macintosh.

In a medium saucepan over medium-low heat, bring ½ cup water to a boil. Add the sugar, lemon juice, and spices, and stir with a wooden spoon until the sugar dissolves. Simmer for 5 minutes to release the flavor of the spices.

Add the apples, cover, and cook, stirring occasionally, until the apples are barely tender, about 10 minutes. Remove from the heat. Either puree the applesauce using a food mill or leave it slightly chunky.

THE LILY FAMILY

Liliaceae,
Amaryllidaceae,
and Asparagaceae

EDIBLE SPECIES:
asparagus, chive,
garlic, leek, onion,
shallot, walking onion

Onions and garlic simmering in a pan form the foundation of many recipes, and cooking would be a very different experience without them. Even though the common onion is readily available in the markets, growing your own—whether a clump of chives or a row of leeks—is somehow both rewarding and deeply satisfying. There is something about plucking a fresh shallot, slicing an Italian Red Torpedo onion, or glazing cipollini that will make you swoon with pride. The truth is, most alliums (which include onions, garlic, chives, leeks, and shallots) are among the easiest vegetables to grow, and heirlooms offer far more depth than the ordinary grocery-store yellow onion variety available in net bags.

The family called Liliaceae contains plants that evolved 52 million years ago. Some are important ornamental plants grown exclusively for their flowers, some are poisonous if consumed, and others are prized for their culinary qualities. All derive from wild plants that were valued in ancient times by the early Egyptians, Greeks, and Romans.

CARAMELIZED SHALLOT TIMBALES SERVES 8

Shallots transform into sweet custards with the texture of a rich pâté. Make them in a cup, and then flip them out on a plate for a fancy presentation.

1 tablespoon
extra-virgin olive oil

8 medium shallots,
preferably Zebrune
(about 1 pound), peeled
but kept whole

1 cup vegetable broth
or water

1 teaspoon finely chopped
fresh sage

1 tablespoon sugar

1½ tablespoons dry sherry

1 tablespoon unsalted butter,
softened, for the ramekins

1½ cups heavy cream
or crème fraîche

4 large eggs

4 large egg yolks

½ teaspoon sea salt

⅛ teaspoon freshly ground
black pepper

Fresh sage leaves or edible
nasturtiums, for garnish

In a medium skillet, heat the olive oil over low heat. Add the shallots and cook, stirring often, until they are golden brown on all sides, about 30 minutes. Add the broth and chopped sage, and raise the heat to medium. Cook at a rapid simmer, stirring occasionally, until the liquid has evaporated and the shallots are tender, about 10 minutes.

Sprinkle the shallots with the sugar and sauté, occasionally shaking the pan, until the shallots are glazed, about 1 minute. Sprinkle with the sherry. Scrape the shallots and their juices into a food processor or blender, cool slightly, then puree until smooth; there should be about ½ cup shallot puree.

Position a rack in the center of the oven and preheat the oven to 350°F. Lightly butter eight 4-ounce ramekins.

In a bowl using a whisk or in a blender, whip the cream, eggs, yolks, shallot puree, salt, and pepper until well combined. Pour an equal amount (about ½ cup) into each ramekin. Place the ramekins in a large roasting pan and pour enough hot water into the pan to come halfway up the sides of the ramekins. Cover the pan loosely with aluminum foil.

Bake until the custards are set when given a shake, about 20 minutes. Remove from the oven and let stand for 5 minutes. Run a knife around the inside of each ramekin and invert onto a plate to unmold it. If it does not unmold perfectly, spread into shape with a small butter knife or spoon. Chill until ready to serve. Garnish each custard with a small sage leaf or edible flower before serving.

CARAMELIZED LEEK TART

MAKES ONE 9-INCH TART

Because leeks are grown slightly underground, they require careful cleaning under running water to remove soil or sand before cooking. While the leeks sauté, make the crust; the whole dish can come together in less than an hour.

FILLING

2 large heirloom leeks
(about 1 pound),
preferably Blue Solaise,
or 2 large onions

3 tablespoons
extra-virgin olive oil

2 teaspoons light brown sugar

½ teaspoon sea salt

⅛ teaspoon freshly ground
black pepper

2 tablespoons Marsala wine

1 teaspoon finely chopped
fresh thyme

1 tablespoon finely chopped
fresh rosemary, plus whole
leaves for garnish

1 large egg

2 cups fresh ricotta cheese

1 Tart Shell
(recipe follows)

Finely minced garlic,
for garnish

Clean the leeks by slicing them lengthwise and running them under cool water to remove any grit. Pat them dry and cut the white portions and about 1 inch of the greens crosswise into ½-inch slices. The very top dark green part is not as tender; reserve it for soup stock.

In a large skillet, heat the oil over medium-high heat. Add the leeks and cook, stirring often with a wooden spoon to prevent them from burning, until soft, about 15 minutes. Stir in the brown sugar, salt, and pepper. Reduce the heat to low and cook, stirring often, until the leeks are golden brown and have a sticky texture, about 25 minutes. Stir in the Marsala and chopped herbs, and continue to simmer for another 5 minutes, until fragrant.

Position a rack in the center of the oven and preheat the oven to 375°F.

In a medium bowl, beat together the egg and ricotta and transfer the mixture into the pastry shell. Spread the caramelized leeks evenly on top.

Bake for 45 minutes, until the pastry is golden brown. Remove from the oven, sprinkle with garlic and rosemary leaves, and let stand 10 minutes to cool slightly before serving.

TART SHELL

1½ cups unbleached
all-purpose flour,
plus more for rolling

½ teaspoon salt

½ cup (1 stick) unsalted
butter, chilled and cut into
½-inch pieces

½ cup sour cream
or plain yogurt

Blend together the flour and salt in the bowl of a food processor fitted with the steel blade and whir until mixed. With the motor running, add the butter, one piece at a time, taking a few seconds in between additions to allow the butter and flour to fully blend. Stop, add the sour cream all at once, and whir again for about a minute, just until the dough forms a ball; don't overblend.

On a lightly floured work surface, roll the dough into an 11- to 12-inch circle about ⅛ inch thick. Fit it into a 9-inch pie pan, trimming the overhang to ½ inch all around. Fold the edges under and crimp the dough. Refrigerate until ready to use.

ROASTED ASPARAGUS
with Spring Mushrooms   Serves 4

There's nothing like fresh asparagus to announce spring. Roasting asparagus spears, a variation on the traditional steamed preparation, creates a sweet caramelized flavor.

12 to 15 spears (1 pound) fresh asparagus, preferably Mary Washington, peeled and tough stem ends trimmed

2 tablespoons (¼ stick) unsalted butter

1 tablespoon extra-virgin olive oil

½ cup fresh shiitake mushrooms, destemmed and sliced, or other mushrooms, sliced or left whole if small

¾ cup chopped shallots

Sea salt and freshly ground black pepper, to taste

Signet marigolds or lemon wedges, for garnish

Preheat the oven to 450°F. In a shallow 6 × 12-inch baking dish, spread the asparagus in a single layer.

In a small saucepan over low heat, melt the butter and oil together. Add the mushrooms and shallots, and sauté until golden, about 5 minutes.

Scoop up the mushrooms and shallots with a slotted spoon, evenly spread them over the asparagus, and pour the butter-oil evenly over the asparagus. Season with salt and pepper. Roast for 5 minutes, turn the asparagus over once, and spoon the butter and drippings on top. Roast on the other side until tender, about 5 minutes more. Garnish with edible flowers or lemon wedges and serve hot.

HEIRLOOM CULTIVARS IN THE LILY FAMILY

ASPARAGUS: *Conover's Colossal, Mary Washington, Martha Washington*

GARLIC: *Porcelain, Samarkand, Early Purple Italian, German Red, Georgian Fire, Chesnok, Broadleaf Czech, Amish Rocambole, Vietnamese Red, Spanish Roja*

LEEK: *Giant Mussleburgh, Blue Solaise, King Richard, Lyon Prizetaker, Saint Victor, American Flag*

ONION

RED: *Red Creole, Red of Florence, Wethersfield Red, Crimson Forest Bunch, Red Welsh Bunching, Red Torpedo (Tropeana Lunga)*

WHITE: *Ailsa Craig, Brunswick, Southport White Globe, cipollini, Flat of Italy, He Shi Ko Bunching, Ishikura Bunching, Yellow Danvers*

MEET THE LILY FAMILY

ASPARAGUS

Asparagus has been grown in North American gardens since the seventeenth century, but it originated in Europe. Asparagus is grown from crowns rather than seeds, and it takes several years after planting before the spears are ready to harvest. Once established, however, the plant can last for up to twenty years. Mary Washington and Martha Washington varieties were once the only types available; because they produce both female and male plants, they will result in a less satisfactory asparagus bed than one planted with hybrids, bred to produce only male plants.

GARLIC

Break open a garlic head and push the cloves into soft ground; it is that easy to grow garlic. Garlic is a long-season crop, however, and takes a year to fully form a head underground, sending up tall green shoots and twisty seed heads known as garlic scapes. Red-skinned garlic is stronger in flavor than white, and Nubia Red, also known as aglio rosso di Nubia, is an Ark of Taste variety from the Sicilian province of Trapani, Italy. With deep purple cloves and a pink outer layer, it is proven to contain a significantly higher quantity of the healthy compound called allicin than other garlic varieties.

BUNCHING OR MULTIPLYING ONION

Similar to scallions yet stronger in flavor, bunching onions are grown primarily for their leaves rather than their roots. Welsh onions are a type of onion called a multiplier, which means they produce a clump of plants that are separated and then replanted to keep them going as a perennial crop.

RED ONION

Red onions are common, but an Italian specialty known as Rossa Lunga di Firenzi is pungent yet sweetly flavored; it is originally from Tropea, a Calabrian town in Italy known for its superb cuisine. Pull as scallions or leave alone to develop into an elongated bulb that can be woven with other bulbs into a beautiful braid to hang in the kitchen near the stove.

TOP-SETTING WALKING ONION

The name "walking onion" comes from the way the onion sets seed on the top of the stem, then topples over when it is ripe. The seeds will root back into the soil by gradually "walking" across the garden and continue growing new plants. Harvest the small top-setting onion bulblets to use for cooking as you would shallots or garlic, and keep the plants growing in the ground.

SHALLOT

Shallots are less strong-tasting than garlic yet more pungent than onions, adding a distinctive quality to any dish. Often pricey at markets yet very easy to grow, one shallot will grow into a half dozen or more bulblets. Save a few bulbs over the winter to replant the following spring for a continuous crop.

THE MINT FAMILY

Lamiaceae

EDIBLE SPECIES:
anise hyssop, basil, lavender, lemon balm, marjoram, mint, oregano, perilla (shisho), rosemary, sage, thyme

The mint family contains a wide range of culinary herbs and aromatics that are used medicinally and for seasoning. This family of plants is a lot less fussy than most vegetables or flowers when it comes to specific growing requirements.

Recognized by common features—square stems and diminutive clustering flowers—most of the plants in this family are still relatively wild, with somewhat aggressive and vigorous root systems that border on invasive. All are exceptionally pollinator-friendly, which should be an open invitation to any landscape or garden.

BASIL PESTO SWIRL ROLLS MAKES 24

A favorite for picnic or potluck, these rolls are always a hit. If you are short on time, skip the bread-making step and buy ready-made pizza dough, although the results won't be quite as tasty.

1 (0.25-ounce) envelope
active dry yeast
(2¼ teaspoons)

1½ cups warm water
(105°F to 115°F)

1 teaspoon sugar

4 tablespoons (½ stick)
unsalted butter,
melted and cooled

4 cups all-purpose
white flour, plus more
for the work surface

1 cup whole-wheat
pastry flour

2 teaspoons sea salt

Olive oil or soft butter,
for greasing the bowl
and pans

1 cup Basil Pesto
(recipe follows)

Maldon flaky salt,
for garnish

Pour the yeast into a large mixing bowl. Stir in the warm water and sugar (which feeds the yeast) and allow it to sit for 10 minutes. Stir in the butter, then both flours and the sea salt, until well blended. (This may also be done in a stand mixer using a dough hook.) Turn the mixture out onto a floured surface and knead until smooth and elastic, adding more flour if the dough is sticky, about 10 minutes.

Place the dough in a lightly oiled bowl, turn once so both sides are oiled, and cover with a moistened tea towel. Allow the dough to rise in a warm place until doubled in size, about 1 hour. Punch the dough down and allow it to rest for 10 minutes.

Lightly oil two 12-cup muffin pans.

Divide the dough in half and, on a lightly floured work surface, roll out each half into a 12 × 8-inch rectangle. Spread each piece of dough evenly with ½ cup pesto. Starting with one long end, roll up each piece of dough jelly-roll-style; set it seam-side down. Using a sharp knife, cut each jelly roll into 1-inch-thick rounds. Place each round in an oiled muffin cup, cut side up. Let the pan stand in a warm place, covered with the tea towel, until the rounds are almost double in size, about 30 minutes.

Meanwhile, preheat the oven to 400°F.

Bake the rolls until golden brown, about 20 minutes. Cool slightly, then remove from the muffin pan onto a cooling rack. Sprinkle with the flaky salt and serve warm.

BASIL PESTO

Makes 1 cup

¼ cup walnuts, lightly toasted
in a dry skillet

2 garlic cloves,
coarsely chopped

2 cups packed fresh
sweet basil leaves,
preferably Genovese,
rinsed and dried

1 cup packed fresh Italian
flat-leaf parsley leaves

½ teaspoon coarse sea salt

¼ teaspoon freshly ground
black pepper

¼ cup freshly grated
Parmigiano-Reggiano cheese

½ cup extra-virgin
olive oil

Combine the walnuts, garlic, basil, parsley, salt, and pepper in the bowl of a food processor and puree until blended. Add the cheese and pulse to combine. With the motor running, add the oil in a slow, steady stream to make a creamy paste.

HEIRLOOM CULTIVARS IN THE MINT FAMILY

BASIL: *Piccolo Fino Verde, Genovese, opal, lemon, cinnamon, Mammoth, Thai*

BEE BALM: *monarda, Oswego tea, bergamot*

LAVENDER: *English (Lavandula angustifolia), which includes Hidcote and Munstead; Spanish (L. stoechas); French (L. dentata)*

LEMON BALM: *Melissa officinalis*

MINT: *chocolate mint, pineapple mint, spearmint, apple mint*

SAGE: *common, Tricolor, Berggarten*

THYME: *common, lemon, woolly, creeping*

LEMON VERBENA–INFUSED PANNA COTTA SERVES 4

Panna cotta, Italian for "cooked cream," is infused with any aromatic herb that appeals, such as lavender or fresh mint. It's best made one to two hours before serving to properly chill.

2½ cups heavy cream

½ cup lemon verbena leaves
(about 12 leaves)

½ cup sugar

1 vanilla bean, split
lengthwise, or 1 teaspoon
vanilla extract

1 (0.25-ounce) packet
powdered gelatin
(about 2 teaspoons)

3 tablespoons cold water

1 cup fresh raspberries,
blueberries, or sliced
strawberries

1 lemon,
zested and juiced

In a medium saucepan over low heat, combine the cream with the lemon verbena. Slowly whisk in the sugar to dissolve, which takes about 2 minutes. Turn off the heat. Scrape the seeds from the vanilla bean into the cream as well as the bean pod, or add the vanilla extract. Cover and let the mixture infuse for 30 minutes. Pour through a strainer to remove the vanilla bean and the lemon verbena leaves. Gently rewarm the infused cream to lukewarm, about 60°F, being careful not to let it come to a boil.

In a separate bowl, sprinkle the gelatin over the cold water and let stand for 5 minutes. Whisk the warm cream into the gelatin and whip until the gelatin is completely dissolved, about 1 minute.

Divide the infused cream evenly among 4 individual ovenproof cups or ramekins. Transfer to the refrigerator and chill for 1 hour, or longer for a firmer custard.

Meanwhile, in a small bowl, toss the berries with the lemon zest and juice.

To serve, run a sharp knife around the edge of each ramekin and invert to unmold each custard onto a serving plate. Serve berries alongside.

MINT GRANITA SERVES 4

Granita does not require a fancy ice cream maker. It is more like a flavored ice, served between courses to refresh the palate, or, as they do in France and Italy, as a refreshing breakfast with brioche. Chocolate mint is a type of peppermint with just a hint of chocolate flavor undertones.

1 cup whole fresh chocolate mint leaves, plus fresh sprigs for garnish

1 cup superfine sugar

Juice of 1 lemon

Chill a 9 × 13-inch metal baking pan and a large metal serving spoon in the freezer for about 30 minutes.

Coarsely chop the mint leaves by hand, transfer them to a food processor along with the sugar, and whir the mixture until it forms a green paste, about 30 seconds.

Add the lemon juice and pulse to combine, scraping down the sides of the bowl as needed. Add 3 cups water and pulse until the sugar dissolves, about 1 minute.

Strain the minty liquid through a fine-mesh sieve into the chilled pan, discarding the solids left behind in the sieve. Freeze the mixture uncovered until it sets around the edges, about 1 hour, depending on your freezer's temperature.

Using the chilled metal spoon, mix the frozen edges into the center, leaving the spoon in the pan to stay cold. Freeze again and repeat the stirring procedure about every 30 minutes, until the mixture has a slushy consistency, 2 to 3 hours total.

Spoon the granita into chilled glasses and garnish each with a mint sprig. Serve immediately.

HERB-SALTED ROAST CHICKEN

SERVES 4

This chicken makes the most of sea salt and a mixture of dried herbs known as herbes de Provence, which in France is generously used in everything from roast chicken to omelets. Make your own herb salt with a light touch of lavender added at the end to accentuate the flavors.

1 (5- to 6-pound)
free-range roasting chicken

½ cup Fresh Herb Salt
(recipe follows)

4 fresh thyme sprigs

4 fresh tarragon sprigs

4 fresh sage sprigs

4 lemons

2 tablespoons (¼ stick)
unsalted butter, melted

4 garlic heads,
halved crosswise

2 tablespoons
extra-virgin olive oil

Position a rack in the lower third of the oven and preheat the oven to 375°F.

Rinse the chicken inside and out, and remove the giblets and any excess fat from the cavity end; pat the outside dry. Place the chicken in a large roasting pan, pat the inside dry, and liberally salt the inside with 2 to 3 tablespoons of the herb salt. Stuff the cavity with the thyme, tarragon, and sage.

Puncture 2 lemons with a small knife in as many places as you can, about 30 holes per lemon. Insert these lemons into the cavity of the chicken and tie the legs together with kitchen twine; tuck the wing tips under the body of the chicken.

Brush the outside of the chicken all over with the melted butter. Sprinkle on the remaining herb salt to cover the bird evenly. Slice the remaining 2 lemons and scatter them and the garlic around the base of the roasting pan. Drizzle the oil over the garlic. Place the pan in the oven and roast the chicken for 1½ hours; every 30 minutes or so, open the oven door, pull out the rack, and baste the chicken by spooning the juices over the skin.

To test the doneness of the chicken, wiggle the drumstick to see if it moves easily, or test with a meat thermometer to register at 165°F. Remove the chicken from the oven, cover with aluminum foil, and allow it to rest for 10 to 15 minutes. Transfer the chicken to a serving platter and thinly slice the meat; start by removing the legs and thighs and then slice the breast. Serve each piece of chicken with a spoonful of the herb-infused juices over the top and some of the baked garlic squeezed out of the soft centers.

FRESH HERB SALT

Makes 1 cup

2 plump garlic cloves,
crushed

½ cup coarse sea salt

1 cup fresh herbs
(equal parts parsley, sage,
rosemary, and thyme)

¼ teaspoon dried
culinary lavender

Chop the garlic and the salt together by hand, blending them thoroughly. Add the fresh herbs and continue to hand chop them into the mixture. Spread the mixture out on a flat baking sheet or wooden cutting board to sit for at least 24 hours, or until the salt has completely dried the herbs. Crush the mixture with your fingers into small pieces or transfer it to a food processor fitted with the steel blade and chop until fine. Transfer to a glass jar with a lid, mix in the lavender, and store at room temperature for up to a year.

ACKNOWLEDGMENTS

Writing *The New Heirloom Garden* has been a pleasure. It would not have happened without the collective vision and generosity of those who contributed to this book you now hold in your hands.

First, I thank editor Dervla Kelly for her enthusiasm and vision. Her patience and dedication were invaluable. Thanks also to editorial assistant Katherine Leak, production editorial director Mark McCauslin, and production manager Phil Leung, who were helpful during times of reorganization.

The Random House–Rodale art team deserve praise for their creativity, starting with Marysarah Quinn and Ian Dingman. From the beginning they determined the design and applied a modern twist to an old-fashioned theme. To accomplish this task they enlisted book designer Catherine Casalino, who created an elegant book layout that surpassed my expectations.

I am grateful to my agent, Angela Miller, for her unflagging faith that this book would come together, and her willingness to be engaged in the process.

Without the extraordinary photographer Matthew Benson, whose magnificent images grace these pages, this would be an entirely different book. He brought humor and spontaneity to the set, approaching each shot with fresh perspective and knowledge of plants. Along with his partner, Jill Rowe, they allowed the photo team to take over their kitchen and barn at Stonegate Farm as a meeting place, and to scour their botanical garden for edible flowers and herbs for suitable garnish.

I consider myself fortunate to have worked on a second book project with food stylist Nora Singley, who is a true artist, along with her cooking assistant, Alyssa Kondracki. They both steadfastly prepared each recipe with precision. Thank you to prop stylist Maeve Sheridan, who brought exquisite plates, bowls, and utensils to the set. As always, Cameron Howard served as my primary recipe tester, and has been at my side ever since my first cookbook in 2003. It was a pleasure to be in the company of imaginative food professionals.

We were fortunate to shoot all the opening pages about the plant families on location at Diana McCargo's and Peter Swift's Philo Ridge Farm in Charlotte, Vermont. Their generosity included a quintessential farmhouse for on-site photography and a plethora of vegetables harvested each day by a farm crew. Equally generous was Josh Carter at Shelburne Farms, who allowed us to glean his field for late-season chard, carrots, winter squash, and alliums.

With gratitude and love, I wish to thank my friends Deborah Riemar for reading and editing, Randall Perkins for design consultation, Margot Page for sculpting my original proposal, Thomas Henry Pope for seed-saving expertise, and gardening friends Page Dickey, Kathy LaLiberte, and Sally Ferguson. There are so many others who have inspired me over the years with their gardens.

To my good friends who have been on this journey with me for the past several years, thank you for coming together in my garden and at my table.

INDEX

RECIPE INDEX

All rights reserved.
Published in the United States by Rodale Books,
an imprint of Random House, a division
of Penguin Random House LLC, New York.
rodalebooks.com

RODALE and the Plant colophon
are registered trademarks of
Penguin Random House LLC.

Library of Congress Cataloging-in-
Publication Data is available.

ISBN 978-1-63565-083-9
Ebook ISBN 978-1-63565-084-6

Printed in China

Book and cover design by Catherine Casalino
Book and cover photographs by Matthew Benson
Illustrations by Terry Findeisen

10 9 8 7 6 5 4 3 2 1

First Edition